further praise for

Marzahn, Mon Amour

“Katja Oskamp knows how to capture the essence of people beautifully. They really come to life in her portraits. A powerful book.”

Frank-Walter Steinmeier, President of Germany

“A real gem… full of tough wit and resilience.”

Catherine Taylor, *The Irish Times*

“Charming”

Exberliner

“It’s rare to come across a book of such captivating warmth and humour. There is something magical at play in *Marzahn, Mon Amour*. I loved every page of it.”

Rónán Hession, author of *Leonard and Hungry Paul* and *Panenka*

“*Marzahn, Mon Amour* captures a piece of modern history and brings it right down to the human level.”

Catherine Venner, *World Literature Today*

“Bereavement, suicide, addiction and disability are just some of the themes explored in this absorbingly intimate novella. From the humdrum to the dramatic, it offers a fascinating window into daily life and a touching tribute to Marzahn and its inhabitants.”

European Literature Network

“A rich reflection on the [illegible] re of community in a neigh[illegible] ble.”

[illegible] *ction*

AUTHOR

Katja Oskamp was born in 1970 in Leipzig and grew up in Berlin. After completing her degree in theatre studies, she worked as a playwright at the Volkstheater Rostock and went on to study at the German Literature Institute in Leipzig. Her debut collection of stories, *Halbschwimmer*, was published in 2003. In 2007 she published her first novel, *Die Staubfängerin*. *Marzahn, Mon Amour*, published by Hanser with the subtitle 'A Chiropodist's Tales', was selected for the 'Berlin Reads One Book' campaign and thus literally became the talk of the town. She is a member of PEN Centre Germany. *Marzahn, Mon Amour* is her first work to be translated into English.

TRANSLATOR

Like the narrator in *Marzahn, Mon Amour*, Jo Heinrich found her ideal career in her middle years, and graduated in 2018 with a distinction in her MA in Translation from the University of Bristol. She was shortlisted for the 2020 Austrian Cultural Forum London Translation Prize and the 2019 John Dryden Translation Competition. She translates from French and German, and she lives just outside Bristol with her family. *Marzahn, Mon Amour* is her first literary translation.

MARZAHN, MON AMOUR

Katja Oskamp

Translated from the German by Jo Heinrich

PEIRENE

First published in Great Britain in 2022 by
Peirene Press Ltd
6 Trim Street
Bath, Somerset, England, BA1 1HB
www.peirenepress.com

First published under the original German title *Marzahn, mon amour: Geschichten einer Fußpflegerin* in 2019 by Carl Hanser Verlag, Munich, Germany.

ISBN 978-1-908670-69-4

The translation of this work was supported by a grant from the Goethe-Institut.

Designed by Sacha Davison Lunt
Typeset by Tetragon, London
Printed and bound in Great Britain by Clays Ltd, Elcograf S.p.A.

The content of this book represents the views of the author only and is her sole responsibility. The European Commission and the Agency do not accept any responsibility for use that may be made of the information it contains.

For Doris and Hartmut Eisenschmidt,
my parents

The middle years, when you're neither young nor old, are fuzzy years. You can no longer see the shore you started from, but you can't yet get a clear enough view of the shore you're heading for. You spend these years thrashing about in the middle of a big lake, out of breath, flagging from the tedium of swimming. You pause, at a loss, and turn around in circles, again and again. Fear sets in, the fear of sinking halfway, without a sound, without a cause.

I was forty-four years old when I reached the middle of the big lake. My life had grown stale: my offspring had flown the nest, my other half was ill and my writing, which had kept me busy until then, was more than a little iffy. I was carrying something bitter within me, completing the invisibility that befalls women over forty. I didn't want to be seen, but nor did I want to see. I'd had it with people, the looks on their faces and their well-meant advice. I sank to the bottom.

On 2 March 2015, a few days after my forty-fifth birthday, I packed some clothes, shoes, towels and a fitted sheet into a large bag and took it across Berlin, from Friedrichshain to Charlottenburg. I was afraid I might bump into my literary agent when I came out of the S-Bahn station, as her office was nearby. Recently, she'd passed on nothing but rejections: my novella had been turned down by twenty publishers. I took a few detours and tiptoed around a few corners, but it was much too early for her to be out. When I reached the house at number 6, there were other women standing by the entrance, also with big bags or wheeled cases. Women like me, no younger, no slimmer. Hesitantly, I asked if I was in the right place. They nodded. We smiled weakly: yes, me too, trying out something new again, who knows if it's the right move? I smoked a cigarette with a careworn doctor's receptionist from Spandau, and then it was time to go inside. The lift could only hold two people. We all took the stairs; each floor led to another. By the top floor, the legion of women were panting under the weight of their baggage. Another woman stood in the doorway, tall and thin, dressed in white.

'Gitta,' she introduced herself without smiling, giving each of us her scrawny hand. 'Get changed and spread your sheets over the chairs. Make sure you cover the armrests.'

We crowded into the changing corner and unpacked our things, careful not to take up too much space. We were ashamed of our ageing bodies as we cast off our dark trousers for white ones. We stretched our sheets over the chairs and clumsily lined up. We were desperate not to make a mistake. We were back in the classroom: we had signed up for the Chiropody A course at a school for healthcare and beauty professionals which pretentiously called itself an academy. Gitta was our teacher.

We made a lot of mistakes. We forgot to examine each other's feet, we forgot the towels for our laps, we forgot the cushions for behind the knees. We mixed up our claw toes and our hammer toes, our cuticle nippers and our nail clippers, our disinfecting solution and our alcohol. We were sloppy with the hygiene procedures. We wasted our cuticle softener, put our scalpels together wrong, unable to fit the blades to the handles properly. We were too careful, too brutal, too thorough, too hasty, too slow, too quick. We hurt each other. Sometimes someone would start bleeding and would need to be patched up. We forgave each other for everything. When we couldn't answer Gitta's questions, we hummed and hawed ineptly, like losers, fakes and idiots. Her sharp voice made our necks tense up.

At break times we went downstairs, stood in front of number 6, ate our sandwiches and smoked.

One of the women was a blonde from Eastern Europe who wore sweaters interwoven with gold. She had the loveliest uniform out of all of us, a tunic with a cinched waist and diagonally arranged buttons. Her mascaraed eyelashes curled upwards and her contact lenses gave her blue eyes a shimmering sparkle. Glamour Puss had come here for a break from the adolescent brood eating her out of house and home, and maybe also because of her own worn-out feet. She'd gone through three pregnancies in her high heels. She originally came from Georgia but had been living in a town in the Erzgebirge Mountains for years. Every morning she spent three hours on the train to Berlin, then three hours getting back in the evenings. Anything was better than sitting around at home, she said, and now her son was fifteen she could leave the local man she'd married. When I told her how good her German was, she said she used to work as a translator. Another time she showed us her tongue, which had a piece missing 'from tongue cancer'.

The careworn doctor's receptionist from Spandau worked full-time and had taken time off to complete the course. Her fourteen-year-old son was suffering from a rare, incurable illness that made him more and more immobile the older and bigger he got. Soon she would no longer be able to carry him, and the painkillers she took for her back had already ceased to have any effect. In two years, her boss would be retiring and she wanted to be self-employed by then. Whether she would have her own practice or stay at home with her son remained to be seen.

Then came the patients: mostly elderly people who were giving up three hours of their day to get their feet looked after for free by unskilled novices. I saw beads of sweat on Glamour Puss's forehead, her hair in a net, her eyes behind protective goggles, the lower half of her face behind her white mask, as if she was going into battle. I saw the blade tremble in the careworn receptionist's gloved hand, before she hacked at a patient's heel until it bled. I saw Glamour Puss's blue eyes water from the smell of a severe fungal nail infection. We hunched over and tensed up, Gitta's sharp eye always over our shoulders, her sharp finger at our weak points and her sharp criticism in our ears, which glowed red with trepidation.

None of us had taken a direct path; all of us were on the rebound from somewhere, stranded or bogged down. We knew what failure felt like. We had arrived humble, modest and subdued, ready to forget our previous lives, erase our accomplishments and start again with clean slates. We had reached a low point, at people's feet, and even there we were failing. Gitta didn't make a note of our names. We would disappear; the next lot would come, women like us, middle-aged mothers, eager and obedient, nameless players in a nameless midfield, relegated to the footnotes of our own lives.

At home I learned the names of the twenty-six bones in the foot by heart and studied nail structure, foot deformities and the causes and symptoms of thrombosis. I memorized the materials that burr heads come in, the effects of herbal medicines, types of skin cancer, the difference between viruses, bacteria and fungal spores, the specific problems affecting diabetic feet and terminology like 'fissures', 'rhagades' and 'varicose veins'. My partner would test me in the evenings as we lay in bed, buried under paper covered in notes and drawings of feet.

We took our written theory test in the attic of number 6. A doctor came to the academy to mark the practical test. We all passed – Glamour Puss on her second attempt. We were relieved and even proud. Gitta presented us with certificates and shook hands with each of us. She smiled. She had been a good teacher. After a coffee near Charlottenburg S-Bahn station, we went our separate ways, parting with a wistful sadness. I don't know what became of the other women.

When you've become invisible you can do terrible things, wonderful things, peculiar things. No one sees you doing them. At first, I didn't tell anyone about my decision to retrain. But afterwards, when I was swanning around with my certificate, I came up against revulsion, incomprehension and, the hardest to bear, sympathy. From writer to chiropodist – what a spectacular comedown. I had forgotten how much people, the looks on their faces and their well-meant advice, got on my nerves.

I wasn't going to wait around for them. I had two strong hands that could do a worthwhile job. It wouldn't be an easy start, but it would be glorious, like all beginnings.

You're at an age when your child's youth takes you back to your own, but your partner's illness has turned you from lover into carer. Surfacing in the middle of the big lake and swimming on, there's plenty you can see, plenty you are familiar with and even more you can imagine. You're at an age when, if you're at the start of an adventure, thoughts of how it will end are already creeping in on the quiet. My middle years, working as a chiropodist in Marzahn, will have been good years.

FRAU GUSE

I take the M6 tram east, fourteen stops to the outskirts of Berlin. The journey lasts twenty-one minutes. I get off and immediately register the difference in temperature. As always, the weather here in Marzahn, once the biggest expanse of *plattenbau* prefab tower blocks in the former East Germany, seems more intense than in the centre. The seasons have more of a smell about them.

Our beauty salon is less than two minutes' walk from the tram stop. We have our ground-floor location to thank for so many of our clients with crutches, walking frames and wheelchairs. I look up, struck as always by the sense of being dwarfed by the eighteen storeys bearing down on the salon. Here, at the foot of this enormous building, is where I do my chiropody.

I change into my white work clothes, take my sandwiches to the kitchen, make myself a coffee, get my room ready and check the diary to see if anyone has cancelled or booked a last-minute appointment.

And then the doorbell rings. Quarter to ten. I hurry to the entrance, turn the sign from 'Closed' (red) to 'Open' (green), unlock the door and exclaim, 'Frau Guse! Step inside!'

Frau Guse parks her walking frame and hangs her jacket on the coat stand, breathing heavily. She waddles into the chiropodist's room with her shopping bag and sits down on the chiropody chair. I help her take off her shoes and socks and roll up her trouser legs. Together we lower her feet into the footbath I've prepared. I pluck two gloves from their box and slip them on, turning to Frau Guse, who mentions, as she does at this point every time, that she had breast cancer. I nod and say, as I do at this point every time, that her operation was almost seven years ago and that the tablets she's had to take ever since have terrible side effects, such as shortness of breath and diarrhoea. To a novice who doesn't know any better, it may sound crazy that I'm listing back the ailments Frau Guse is clearly already familiar with, but the professional knows that the exchange of information makes up merely a fraction of all communication, the vast majority of which is something else altogether, and Frau Guse and I are playing around with this vast majority in perfect harmony. When I drop the perfectly timed keyword of diarrhoea, she says, just as expected, that sometimes she doesn't even dare leave the house for fear of messing her trousers. Frau Guse and I could even swap lines; I certainly know both parts off by heart, as we have exactly the same conversation every six weeks.

That's too bad, I reply, and Frau Guse nods, and she smiles the delightfully crooked smile she always surprises and impresses me with when she's on the more lurid subjects. And then she says, as if she's never said it before, 'Ever since the operation... since the operation, only since the operation...

I never had that problem before, just since the operation… nothing before, just since the operation.'

At this point, as she sees me rubbing the foot scrub between my palms, she puts her own towel in her lap, distinguishing herself as a true regular who always brings a towel from home. This, of course, elicits my praise. As I tell her that we – my colleagues and I – are grateful for this kind assistance from our clientele, which helps us keep down the mountain of washing, we shift gracefully from illnesses to housekeeping. I bow down before Frau Guse and the footbath, and I need only to open my hands for Frau Guse to lift her left foot out of the water and hold it aloft for me. I work on her heel, sole, arch and instep, going between her toes with my fingers, scrubbing off the dead skin, as Mary Magdalene once did with Jesus's feet. Biblical themes don't necessarily enter my conversation with Frau Guse; nor do I dry her feet with my hair as Mary did, using instead the towel she brought with her to dry them thoroughly.

'You can sit back and relax now,' I say, which means Frau Guse can let out a blissful sigh. She does this as scheduled, before moving on with that crooked smile to the breast prosthesis that she owns but never uses. We skim over illnesses again before I gallantly move things along by complimenting her on her floaty blouse, which drapes so lightly you'd never get an inkling of her missing breast. Oh yes, Frau Guse confides, lowering her eyelids coquettishly, she likes to wear loose, light clothes with plenty of colour. Then comes the moment when I crown my client as queen, at last: I step on the pedal and, with a low hum, Frau Guse, along with her pink throne of a chair, rises up, framed against a backdrop of white walls, making us joke every time that she might go through the ceiling. I roll my cabinet closer, switch on the magnifying lamp, adjust its pivoting arm so the light glares down on Frau Guse's feet and then, once she has reached the heights of royalty, I, as her servant, take my seat, wheeling my white stool under my bottom. Goggles on and down to business. The nippers come out first, for her thicker nails.

'If it hurts—' I say.

'I'll let you know,' Frau Guse says.

Then I move on to her involuted nails, which are in danger of growing into the skin at the sides. I cut off a small corner, reach for a probe and pick out hard dead skin from underneath and from her nail folds. Ten times over, I gently push back the cuticle from the base of her nail. I put a burr into the handpiece, select a low speed and turn the instrument on. There's a buzzing between us, the sound of the motor and the suction; at this point I am just as hard of hearing as my royal client. The noise silences us. I look at Frau Guse over the top of my goggles; she is calmly, quietly smiling her crooked smile.

Born in 1933 in Berlin's Prenzlauer Berg district, left school at fourteen, no professional training. Worked briefly as an untrained cleaner. Married in 1953, five children by 1966. Husband died at forty-five, in 1973. She brought up her children on her own; each learned a trade – bricklaying, metalwork or sales. In 1993 Frau Guse moved from Prenzlauer Berg to Marzahn. She's already paid for her funeral (4,000 euros), chosen her urn (oak-leaf design), picked out the music (*Nabucco*) and leased her cemetery plot, next to her husband.

Frau Guse looks down at her squeaky-clean filed nails with satisfaction. I turn the motor off, put the burr into disinfecting solution, take off my goggles and reach for the hard skin paddle.

The room is quiet again.

'Let's scrape your hooves,' I say.

'I'm not a horse,' says Frau Guse.

I start with the coarse side of the file and Frau Guse helps by holding her feet out like pokers, extending her heels for me. The tiny flakes rain down. Then I turn the file to its finer side. Frau Guse doesn't have a lot of rough skin, as she no longer uses her feet much.

When I ask why her husband died so young, she always says he had a stomach operation. This isn't a cause of death. I can see in her eyes that even today, forty-five years later, she can't understand why he died, and as the years go by, she understands it less and less. She also has trouble listing the names of her five children, but they come to her eventually: Lothar, Bärbel, Joachim, Uwe, Christine. Frau Guse doesn't have dementia. She's just slowly distancing herself and reversing away from the world she used to know her way around – kids, cooking, Kaufhalle for her shopping.

'What's for dinner tonight, Frau Guse?'

'Wouldn't you like to know?'

We giggle. Frau Guse pretends to be mischievous and I pretend to be nosy and impatient. Frau Guse likes a joke.

'Today it's... today I'm making... today I'll get... just after this, once I'm finished here, I'm getting... half a chicken!' she tells me, with an impish tone – she's a smart cookie.

Frau Guse might once have been a good cook but I get the impression that these days her meal plan varies between kebabs, chicken and Chinese. At the weekends, though, she cooks properly, like a good German housewife. And what does she cook? Kassler: in other words, smoked salted pork. It's on Frau Guse's menu every Saturday. She serves it with potatoes and sauerkraut. As for the meat... Here comes my very favourite bit of the whole session.

'In the electric bread slicer... I buy the kassler in one piece and then I slice it in the electric bread slicer... I cut it into lovely slices in the bread slicer... The kassler, yes. That surprised you, didn't it? I do it in the bread slicer.'

'In the bread slicer?' I cry in amazement, utterly taken aback.

'Yes,' she says, haughtily, 'in the bread slicer.'

As we celebrate Frau Guse's kassler-cutting technique to the full, I take the towel and wipe the dust off her heels, which are as smooth as a baby's bottom. Now she has a choice of creams: rose, lavender or maybe propolis? Frau Guse doesn't mind; she leaves it to me. She likes everything to be the same as always. I pump a dollop in my hand and work it into her feet, first the left, then the right. She follows what I'm doing raptly and silently. Then I do something with her feet that no one else has ever done. I stretch her insteps, move her toe joints in a circle one by one, extend her Achilles tendons, clench my fist and push it along her soles, expand her toes and knead her heels.

'You've done a lovely job again.'

We survey my work. Frau Guse is eighty-five; her feet, after the treatment, are now the youngest part of her.

I take my gloves off, bring the throne back down to ground level, draw in the leg rests, fold up the towel and help Frau Guse put her socks and shoes on.

She sways a little as she gets up and holds on tight to the armrest, steadying herself as she stands upright. She takes her shopping bag, slips in her towel and waddles out of the room.

'I need to pay you,' Frau Guse cries.

I pop behind the counter. Frau Guse is great at paying. She can hardly wait to pay up. Unlike modern people who prefer credit, instalments and payment-free months, Frau Guse does her best to avoid running up a debt, owing anything to anyone or leaving any bills unpaid. When she manages this, she is happy, and she pays at the earliest opportunity, preferably before a service is rendered. That's why she has paid for her own funeral. With a childlike pride, she pulls out her purse. I put her twenty-two euros in the till.

HERR PAULKE

When I was starting out at the salon, one of my very first clients was Herr Paulke. In an early session, he asked me with a laugh, 'Do you realize where you are? We're on top of Berlin's shit. There used to be sewage farms here, before they threw up these tower blocks. When they dig the earth up, you can still smell it.'

Herr Paulke moved to the area in 1983, into a brand-new apartment: an original Marzahner, a proletarian. An old man with a heart of gold, he had a fatalistic sense of humour and humility in the face of the havoc old age was wreaking. Herr Paulke didn't take himself too seriously. His face was an asymmetric mishmash of features – crossed eyes, warts, liver spots, crooked tooth implants – a motley collection accrued over the various stages of his life. One of his knees was completely out of action. Osteoarthritis. His feet gave me a fright the first time I washed them in the footbath, but I soon grew to like them. They were swollen all over, their skin discoloured, brown and scaly, etched with a thousand lacy periwinkle-blue veins. Like weathered pebbles.

Herr Paulke used to work for Autotrans, the biggest name in East German haulage. All his life, he lugged around wardrobes, freezers and pianos. As well as run-of-the-mill house removals, his division transplanted whole factories from A to B and accompanied orchestras on guest performances abroad. That had been great, Herr Paulke told me. Every so often he and his colleagues were allowed into the concerts for free, before it was time to clear everything away, load it onto lorries and take it all back home. When Herr Paulke was no longer up to heavy lifting, he was transferred to customer service, to deal with home visits, contracts and estimates. When even that became too much, he asked to work in the office but was turned down. Herr Paulke tightened his belt and took early retirement at fifty-seven. The year 1989 spelled the GDR's demise and, for Herr Paulke, the diagnosis of a lymphoma under the right side of his jaw. He underwent surgery and radiotherapy.

Once his cancer had been brought under control, Herr and Frau Paulke started to travel, twice a year. Looking back on it, Herr Paulke said, with his Berlin accent, 'It was good we seized the chance.' He could talk about the Norwegian fjords, the palm trees in Ticino and the pubs in Dublin. When I first got to know Herr Paulke, though, it had been a long time since he'd been able to travel. He moved within a radius that was growing ever smaller.

Every time I saw Herr Paulke, there was something else that needed repairing. He once told me he'd had 'some kind of pipe' put in his right side, 'from my neck down to my groin, to regulate something – it'll need adjusting every so often'. He didn't fully understand it, but he trusted the consultants. Every time he had to visit the doctor, Frau

Paulke would ring up and book the patients' transport service, usually to take him to the UKB hospital in Marzahn, or the 'UKV', as he sometimes called it by mistake. Only the physiotherapist went to his house, twice a week for twenty minutes. 'She walks me up and down the stairs. I have to do knee bends and then lie on my back and cycle with my legs.' I marvelled at these exercises. 'Yes, yes,' said Herr Paulke with a hint of pride in his voice, 'all that kind of thing.'

When the cancer came back in his lower jaw a year and a half ago, Herr Paulke told me about his forthcoming operation, at the UKB again. 'Are you worried?' I asked, as I was tidying up his feet ready for his stay in hospital. Herr Paulke thought for a moment. 'Well, if it works, it works, and if it doesn't work, it doesn't work.'

Six weeks later he was at the door again, punctual as ever but much thinner. 'The food was crap – nothing but soup for three weeks. I've lost ten kilos. But my toenails have grown.' His toes twitched as I pushed back his cuticles.

'Does it tickle?' I teased.

'So much the better,' Herr Paulke laughed. 'It shows I'm alive!'

In September 2016, Herr Paulke turned up with no teeth; the entire upper row had gone. Where his incisors had been, there were now two shiny dark golden stumps. He wasn't using his temporary dentures because, he said, they rubbed: 'Can't even eat a banana. It sticks under them.'

Whenever I laughed at something that Herr Paulke said in his matter-of-fact way, emotion almost imperceptibly flashed across his face, a mixture of incredulity, pride and shame. He was no longer used to anyone paying him any attention. For a moment, the memory of the young, vibrant man he had once been would come back to him. The man who had flirted with women. He would have known all the moves. He had a good memory.

That September day, I carefully massaged cream into his feet, took my gloves off and helped him with his socks and shoes. He lifted himself off the chair. I held out my hands to him and he took them. Warm, slack skin. We stood like this, our eyes meeting. It was a beautiful moment. We both felt its joy. It did some good, and not just in steadying Herr Paulke's balance. I would have liked to pick a piece of fluff from his shoulder, straighten his collar or briefly stroke his cheek – go beyond my normal services. Herr Paulke smiled, with his lips closed.

'It's been a pleasure as always,' I said.

'For me too,' he replied, casting his eyes downward.

Then he looked over my shoulder, through the window. 'My wife – she's outside.'

He held on to my arm and we shambled into the reception area. I opened the door for Frau Paulke, made a new appointment for Herr Paulke, put his money in the till and thanked him for his tip, generous as ever. I slipped his towel and wallet into the little bag where Frau Paulke kept her diary (actually a thick piece of A4 paper).

'I've bought one for next year,' said Frau Paulke, bemoaning the fact that she was always behind with her appointments. The earliest optician's appointment she could get was three months away. The physiotherapist would be round again tomorrow. Her replacement hip wasn't behaving. She found it hard to get moving in the mornings. She could manage a quick walk on a good day, but her husband could only walk slowly. There was smoked fish on sale at the market. Had I heard that the supermarket nearby was changing hands?

Herr Paulke said his goodbyes and heaved his walking frame out of the door, pushing it with long, lame steps, his knees buckling, his shoulders hunched. Frau Paulke walked alongside him. 'See you in six weeks,' I called out. 'Take care!' Herr Paulke raised a hand. The effort of moving forward was quite enough without turning around as well.

Four weeks later, I had a call from Frau Paulke. Her husband couldn't come to his next appointment: he'd died. Shocked, I passed on my sympathies to her. His new teeth had just arrived, she told me in a fluster, they were in a box on the table in front of her. 'I've got to pay 2,000 euros for them, even though they're of no use to me. It's not even as if anyone else can have them.'

I closed my eyes for a moment. Then I drew a line through Herr Paulke's name in the diary.

I recently bumped into Frau Paulke at the local Netto. I needed bin bags, cotton-wool pads and coffee for the salon. Frau Paulke was looking for frozen mixed vegetables. She looked frail and had a walking stick. I asked her if she ever went to visit her husband at the cemetery. She shook her head. 'It's too far. My son took me once. I sat on a bench there. Oh, and by the way, they were very helpful at the dentist's – I only had to pay 500 euros for his teeth.'

FRAU BLUMEIER

It's hard to shift preconceptions about the prefab housing estates in eastern Berlin. They say Marzahn is a concrete wasteland, but in reality it is exceptionally green. There are wide streets, ample parking spaces, good pavements and dropped kerbs at crossings. If you've got wheels, you can get around just fine.

One preconception, though, does hold true: the *plattenbau* tower blocks aren't soundproofed at all. If someone anywhere in the building turns on a drill, down on the ground floor in the salon we feel like we're at the dentist's.

I've known Frau Blumeier for two and a half years now. She is a funny, lively woman with a Berlin accent who looks younger (mid-fifties) than she is (mid-sixties). She lives in the same block as our salon, on the fourteenth floor. When I stand outside our door smoking, I can sometimes see Frau Blumeier from afar. We wave to each other, then Frau Blumeier turns with her joystick and wheels up to me for a quick chat. After that she has to dash off for her physiotherapy, her shopping, a haircut or to see a friend, all in her racy electric wheelchair, her upper body bent forward like a cyclist and her hair swept back from her forehead by the wind. The top speed of three miles an hour that her wheels can do is too slow for Frau Blumeier. She would much rather go around at four, five or six miles an hour. Frau Blumeier lives in hope of a tailwind, to make her battery last longer.

When she turns up for her appointment every seven weeks, I rush to hold the door open and say, 'Come on in!' and Frau Blumeier quips, 'And sit down, hmm?' She rolls through to the chiropody room, parks near the chair, gets up out of her wheelchair and manages the two or three steps on her crooked legs without my help. Frau Blumeier does everything she can by herself, even the disabled jokes. She has no time for wheelchair users who are waited on hand and foot.

She sits on my throne and I take her cosy little children's slippers off. While I'm washing and drying her feet, we chat about the latest news and have a laugh. Frau Blumeier has a phrase in her repertoire that she uses often, like a magic spell: 'That's just what I was going to say!' Everything I say is something Frau Blumeier was about to say. She was just about to say what other people say as well. This sentence opens doors and paves the way for her. She is the queen of affirmation.

In 1955, when Tine Blumeier was just one, she was diagnosed with poliomyelitis, polio for short, or infantile paralysis. She went into hospital for ventilation in an iron lung and wasn't discharged until she was almost four. At best, she could sit up and eat baby food, but Frau Blumeier only knows this from hearsay. She does, though, remember her father's words: 'You have a few limitations. But you are not ill.' The doctors advised her parents to send her to a special school. They ignored the advice and sent their daughter to a standard GDR secondary school. Apart from sports lessons, Tine Blumeier was able to keep up just fine. She left school, worked as a secretary and got married. The doctors strongly advised her not to get pregnant. In 1990, at the age of thirty-six, Tine Blumeier had a son. That was when the company she worked for went into liquidation. She was told she wouldn't have much chance in the West with her disability. She wasn't in a wheelchair at that point, but she did walk with a stick: the first signs of post-polio syndrome were making themselves known and her muscles were starting to waste away. Then, while her son was going through puberty, his father died of leukaemia. That was a hard time, she says.

When Tine Blumeier, with her high spirits, became one of my regulars, my secret resolution to have every client leave happier than when they arrived was tested to the full. I have around sixty clients and the contrast is striking. Some take every cough or cold as a personal affront, moaning for years on end and feeling horribly cheated by life. But not this queen of affirmation. She told me how once, when she was out, a little boy asked his mother if 'that lady in the wheelchair' was disabled. 'Only my legs, not in my head!' Frau Blumeier had called out, and she'd let the boy have a ride on her lap.

'His mother should be grateful to you,' I said.

'That's just what I was going to say!' said Frau Blumeier.

Whenever she comes to see me, she raves about it – how lovely it is not to have to bother with her feet any more, such an improvement to her life, even her son approves. He actually bought a car so he could take his mother out. Her son is everything to her, and she's still pleased she didn't take the doctors' advice, even if the physical strain of pregnancy may have brought on her post-polio syndrome a few years early.

Another time she told me about a miserable woman she knew who had a really messy apartment. Frau Blumeier would check in on her, do her shopping for her, sort out the post, do the washing. She would walk through the clutter on her crutches, trying to clear a path as she was tidying. But she wouldn't be able to help this weekend, as she was going on a boat trip.

'What sort of boat?' I asked.

'Hmm,' teased Frau Blumeier, 'wouldn't you like to know?'

She'd met up with Lutz, an old friend from her youth, and Lutz was always inviting her to go on his boat. Frau Blumeier and her childhood friend would sail happily across the River Spree together, with a picnic and all the trimmings.

'Are you smitten, Frau Blumeier?'

'That's just what I was going to say!'

Over the next winter Frau Blumeier and Lutz lived it up at the best Christmas markets, a trip every weekend – Nuremberg, Dresden, Lübeck. On my throne, Frau Blumeier would take her legs in both hands, bundle them into position and revel in her foot massage, which, as she had no hard skin, could be more thorough than my usual ones. I would look into her face, which, maybe because of the light layer of fluff on her lip, reminded me a little of a cat. Frau Blumeier would purr.

It's a Wednesday at the beginning of March, just before four o'clock. Frau Blumeier is already giggling as she crosses the salon's threshold. As usual, I'm not allowed to help her out of her wheelchair into the chiropody chair. I take the children's slippers off her feet. We're chatting and joking. As I'm trimming her tiny toenails, Frau Blumeier blurts out, 'Something so embarrassing happened the other day!'

I look up from her toes and their soft skin, which I must take care not to harm.

While they were having sex, the bed collapsed, and she and Lutz were left scrabbling around on the floor, trying to fiddle the slats back onto the frame. The next day, the man who lived in the apartment under hers got in the lift with a stupid grin on his face and said, 'You have a blast at yours at night, don't you?' Frau Blumeier was so embarrassed she could have crawled under a rock. She loves living in Marzahn, but it's outrageous that everyone in the apartment block can hear everything. And the worst thing is that every time she bumps into that man, he'll have that stupid grin on his face – he'll never get over it.

'Frau Blumeier,' I say, 'he's jealous.'

'That's just what I was going to say!' says Frau Blumeier.

HERR PIETSCH

Many people think Marzahn is teeming with former GDR bigwigs and SED party officials. It's not true; I'd stake my life on it, especially as I work here. I look after the feet of former bricklayers, butchers and nurses. There's also a woman who worked in electronics, one who bred cattle and another who was a petrol pump attendant.

There is, though, one dyed-in-the-wool party functionary who visits me regularly. Since I've known him, the stereotype has acquired a name: Herr Pietsch. He is a walking cliché.

Herr Pietsch arrives promptly at the salon door for his appointments, checked flat cap on his bald head, peering imperiously through the window. It is beneath him to knock on a door or ring a bell; a door needs to be opened on Herr Pietsch's arrival. That's what he knows and expects, even if it hasn't been that way for thirty years. I let him in with a 'Greetings, Herr Pietsch', but my smile is not returned. Herr Pietsch silently hangs up his jacket, giving the impression that he's here on official business, to make some kind of inspection. He acknowledges a woman waiting in the wicker chair for her beauty treatment, looking down on her in every sense, given his height. He leads me into the chiropody room, taking his little bag with him.

'How are things with you?' I ask.

Herr Pietsch, taking off his shoes and socks, stares out of the window. By now I know the routine: he is always wary at first, only to drastically overstep the mark later. I bend down, push the footbath into place and look up into his protruding eyes – two bulging orbs. Herr Pietsch speaks with a Thuringian-Saxon accent, a little indistinctly as he's on his third set of teeth: 'There are certainly a few things I'm not happy with, but I'm getting by. I'm on top of life.'

Eberhard Pietsch was born in 1941 into a modest family. He attended a Workers' and Peasants' College, and became a teacher of history and mathematics. He got married and had a daughter. He soon changed tack professionally and started his career as a party official. At first, he ran a branch of the Free German Youth in Thuringia, but before long he was promoted to a party position. He once boasted to me, 'I was the youngest district party secretary in the whole of the GDR!' The district whose party secretary he had been in the 70s bordered West Germany and I was given the impression that Herr Pietsch had guarded all twenty-one miles of the frontier by himself. In 1981 Herr Pietsch moved to the capital with his family, went to conferences in other socialist countries as an SED official, and accompanied GDR delegations to the Olympic Games. I've never found out exactly what his job entailed.

When he first came to see me, he asked me if I knew when the Pioneers' Anniversary was. 'Thirteenth of December,'

I said, and then, on request, recited the dates of National People's Army Day (1 March), Teachers' Day (12 June) and Republic Day (7 October), and I even sang 'May There Always Be Sunshine' in Russian for him, as a little extra. This won me a place in his faltering heart. In me, he sees the diligent young Pioneer I once was. I remind Herr Pietsch of his prime.

While I'm washing his feet, he tells me about a new armchair he's bought. He'll have to wait three months for it to be delivered. As he's already got rid of his old armchair, a camping chair is all he has to sit on for now. I dry his long feet, which hang from long legs, reminding me of a hare's paws. Then I step on the pedal, sending Herr Pietsch skywards with a low hum.

In his prime, Herr Pietsch found himself not only politically and ideologically on the right side, but also on the high ground, to his mind at least. He was a cut above, with others below. It's a concept that, deep down, Herr Pietsch has held on to. As I'm familiar with the special dates and songs, I find myself on the right side in Herr Pietsch's eyes, even if I am just a lowly chiropodist.

In his prime, as an influential man, Herr Pietsch didn't just go away on business, he often played away too: here an ambitious comrade, there an interpreter or a track and field athlete. He had a long-term relationship with his secretary. Herr Pietsch must have kept meticulous records about these affairs, as he once told me the exact number of sexual conquests he'd had in his lifetime (fifty-one), on which I congratulated him, as would be expected of a chiropodist as far as Eberhard Pietsch is concerned.

I get the better of his woody toenails, which are never easy to trim. I run a probe under the edges of his nails. It triggers his nerve endings, making Herr Pietsch's toes twitch every so often. He finds it unpleasant and maintains he has no control over it. The drill starts up with a buzz. I carefully even out the grooves in his nails and try to give the freshly trimmed edges a smooth shape, with only partial success given the brittle material I'm working with.

Herr Pietsch had just begun an affair with a buxom party colleague fourteen years his junior when the truth came out. His wife caught him in the act, washed her hands of him and threw him out of the marital home. At the time, not only Herr Pietsch's honour but also the GDR was on its last legs. The Wall came down, East Germany was no more and Frau Pietsch got her divorce. While all of Berlin celebrated German reunification at the Brandenburg Gate, Herr Pietsch was moving into a one-room apartment in Marzahn, where he still lives (and currently sits on his camping chair). He wanted to get back into teaching, but he was turned down. To avoid unemployment, he started working for an insurance company in an office in Marzahn. He managed a customer base that had been absorbed from the GDR's state insurance scheme. After thirteen years of insurance, Herr Pietsch collapsed in the street. An ambulance. Heart surgery. Five bypasses in eight hours. After rehab, Herr Pietsch retired at sixty-three, on a very much pared-down pension.

While I'm scrubbing the rough skin from Herr Pietsch's withered feet, he talks about his next (and forty-third) hike with his cardiac rehab group, in which he takes a leading role. Herr Pietsch plans the hikes: he walks them in advance, times them, tests out the train connections and, once he has counted the names on the list he's passed round, books a table at an inn so the group can refuel and revive themselves at the end of their hike. If it's someone's birthday, Herr Pietsch prepares a speech to give to the group.

I interject to say that the cardiac rehab group must be happy that Herr Pietsch always organizes these hikes to perfection. Unexpectedly, Herr Pietsch isn't pleased with my compliment, raising his brows over his bulbous eyes dismissively and retorting in his broad Saxony accent, '*Bassema off Mädschn*' – in other words, 'Look here, young lady!' This kicks off an explanation that goes right back to basics, a wily fox telling a mentally underdeveloped creature that he can plan these hikes at the drop of a hat, thanks to his years of experience as a district party secretary.

Herr Pietsch spells it out for me, almost as if I should be taking notes: 'I, Eberhard Pietsch, have always been able to organize anything! I, Eberhard Pietsch, know what the cardiac rehab group needs! I, Eberhard Pietsch, am good at public speaking!'

Herr Pietsch has been living alone for almost thirty years. His relationship with his ex-wife is chilly and even his daughter keeps contact to a minimum. Herr Pietsch isn't invited round for family birthdays. No one rings up every once in a while to find out how he is. Herr Pietsch signed over his garden plot to his grandson. The grandson took it on without a word of thanks and still never calls.

I rub the dust from Herr Pietsch's feet and reach for the cream. His skin absorbs it like a sponge and I need to top it up several times. Herr Pietsch starts on his illnesses and doesn't register his foot massage at all. He's lost contact not only with his relatives, but also with his feet. I could be poking in his ears for all the notice he takes.

He talks of the cardiologist, the orthopaedist, the ophthalmologist and the dermatologist, and finally reaches the urologist, whom he visits intermittently for monitoring purposes. Her routine question about his sexual activity forms the transition to Herr Pietsch's central theme: erections, or, more specifically, his erections, which he goes on to describe in detail as attainable, although unreliable. Like the GDR, like his marriage and like his career, Herr Pietsch's erections are leaning towards a sudden collapse. He worries about the medication he's taking for his heart, but nevertheless wants to try out the tablets the urologist recommends for keeping it up. There's just one thing missing: a sexual partner. No sign of one, for miles. Then Herr Pietsch asks me if I might be interested in having sex with him. I tell him I'm already taken; he'll have to make do with a pedicure. But Herr Pietsch sticks to his guns. He says that I'm not stupid and that I have an 'erudite' air about me. I politely turn him down again. Despite, or maybe because of, his defeat, Herr Pietsch straightens himself up and says rather contritely that we'll move on from that subject now. Of course – he still needs to give the orders.

I put his socks back on, unroll his trouser legs, bring the chiropody chair down to ground level and pass Herr Pietsch the shoehorn. His hare's paws disappear into his shoes.

His meagre pension doesn't allow for any extravagance. He's labelled some envelopes that he keeps in his one-room apartment. He puts money aside in them for bigger expenses: the new armchair, a short trip back to his hometown in Thuringia and, last year, an International Garden Exhibition membership. One of his envelopes is for chiropody. Herr Pietsch first came every six weeks, then every five. Now he stands at the door every four weeks.

As I go to leave the room, with the now cold footbath in my hands, Herr Pietsch whips a mini bottle of Söhnlein Brillant sparkling wine out of his bag and presents me with it: 'Good work, Comrade.' I laugh and thank him for the present. Herr Pietsch puts his arm round my waist. 'Can I have a photo of you?'

'No,' I say, 'no photos, Herr Pietsch.'

His bulbous eyes look sad.

At the till, he tells me off – 'Look here, young lady' – as if I were his incompetent secretary: it can't be that difficult to find a new appointment; I must hurry up, he's got other things he needs to do today. I write the appointment in the diary and on Herr Pietsch's client card, put twenty-two euros in the till, lead him to the door and hold it open. He takes his leave seriously and professionally. The six-foot-three pensioner creeps off, checked flat cap on his bald head, back bent, empty bag in his hand. Oh, Eberhard, you old child of the workers and peasants. All your life, you've mistaken your position for your personality. Give my regards to the cardiac rehab group.

THE RUSSIAN WOMAN

All year round a strong breeze blows through Marzahn. I think it's because of the area's proximity to the flat Brandenburg countryside, where the dreaded winds coming down from Siberia whip across and head straight for Marzahn with uncontrollable force, converging into wind tunnels between the tower blocks and sweeping anything off their balconies – seat cushions, geranium planters, parasols – that keen do-it-yourselfers haven't bolted down.

Now, in May, spring has sprung and it's turning green between the tower blocks. There are cherry trees on the grassy area in front of the salon. In April, they were full of luxuriant white blossom, until the wind scattered the petals over the ground like snowflakes. Soon the cherries will ripen, attracting people, the lighter the better, who clamber around in the branches to gather the free fruit. A pair of doves live here, and in the evenings, once it's dark, brown hares hop through the grass.

Tiffy is my boss and the salon's owner. She's six years older than me and five foot two, with an undercut bob. Everything that happens to Tiffy happens here: she's always at the salon, Monday to Friday, every week, every month, every year. She offers beauty treatments and massages. More often than not, her working day can last from 8 a.m. to 8 p.m., but she'll never get rich from it. Her reward is a jam-packed diary and her satisfied clients.

In springtime, Tiffy and I like to stand in the open door for a moment between appointments. We sip our coffee and lift our faces towards the sun, or watch the passers-by. Tiffy knows many of them by name and exchanges greetings with them: for example, the lesbian couple who often walk their chunky dogs on the grass in front of our salon. Children with school backpacks and PE bags dawdle through the grass; old ladies with walking frames trundle past; office workers lug their shopping home; young women pass by, pushing buggies; and sometimes Frau Blumeier whizzes round the corner in her sleek electric wheelchair and waves to us, the wind in her hair. Tiffy and I give her a friendly wave back, before it's time for our next client. Close the door, back to work, as simple as that.

It was three years ago in May, late one Wednesday afternoon. I swept the chiropody room, then took my instruments out of the disinfecting solution in the bathroom and rinsed them off. I had twenty minutes before my next client was due to arrive. Tiffy was in her room, working on Frau Kunkel, who treated herself to a massage once a week, and I was just taking my instruments back to the chiropody room when there was a thunderous banging on the door. I rushed into the reception area and Tiffy came out as well, cupping massage oil in her hands. Through the window we could see the lesbian couple with their chunky dogs. They were flailing their arms about, their eyes and mouths wide open, their dogs pulling at their leads, up on their back legs, barking. Tiffy opened the door.

'Call an ambulance!' they shouted.

A woman had jumped from the building; the dogs had heard the impact and been upset by it. We ran out of the salon and around the corner, the wind lashing into us. There she was, the woman, lying like a discarded doll at the back of the eighteen-storey block, four or five metres away from the wall, next to a manhole cover. We ran back to the salon and I grabbed the phone, dialled the three numbers, then passed the receiver to Tiffy.

'A woman's just jumped from the tower block,' Tiffy shouted. She gave her name and the salon's address.

Frau Kunkel emerged from the back room in her socks, pulling her sweater on. The three of us ran out of the salon. Tiffy gave us instructions: we weren't to touch anything, we just had to keep passers-by back and redirect them. We stood there at the tower block's corner in the wind – the lesbian couple, two dogs, Frau Kunkel, Tiffy and I. We were about twenty metres from the woman. She lay on her front, slightly bent, one leg at an angle. She was wearing a skirt, but no shoes. One foot was strangely twisted. Her T-shirt had ridden up, revealing her bra clip. Her arms lay loosely by her sides. Her face was hidden under a tangle of curly, dark blonde hair. You could almost believe she was asleep. People brought their shopping along the path that had been trodden across the grass, and we redirected them around the front of the block. If they had children with them, we blocked the view. We kept looking over at the woman, as if we had to guard her.

Tiffy suddenly said, 'She's breathing. She's still breathing!'

I couldn't bear standing there any longer.

'Maybe they can't find us,' I said, and ran to the street.

For a minute or so, which seemed like an hour, I kept a lookout for a vehicle with a blue light. At last I saw one approaching at walking pace. I waved my arms; the ambulance driver flashed his lights twice. I guided him into a side road. Paramedics got out. They asked if I was a nurse, presumably because of my white uniform; I said no. The police drove up. A young policewoman asked if I was OK; I said yes. The police cordoned off the area with tape. A handful of onlookers jostled behind it. The paramedics knelt down next to the woman and gently examined her. I turned away, not wanting to see their faces, which would reveal the facts soon enough. The young policewoman asked the lesbian couple some questions and made notes. They covered the woman with a tarpaulin. It all happened with minimal effort, without a stir, calmly and routinely. The police asked the onlookers, and us, to move on. The small crowd obediently dispersed.

'Bye,' said the lesbians, and walked hesitantly away with their dogs.

My next appointment was with Herr Schwarz, a pot-bellied painter with very rough skin, bad rhagades and a gold chain around his neck. I told him what had just happened. Herr Schwarz said there would always be idiots in this world, then started talking about his forthcoming holiday in Turkey. He was going there to laze around in the sun and get his teeth done on the cheap.

That evening, after our last clients had gone, Tiffy and I cleaned and tidied up, and emptied the till. We got changed, closed the windows, turned off the lights. We left the salon and went to the corner. There was nothing to see: no tape, no bloodstains. We said goodbye. I went to the tram stop, from where I turned around and looked up at the eighteen-storey block. Judging from where she had landed, she hadn't jumped from an apartment but from one of the little balconies anyone could reach from the stairwells. Or maybe she hadn't jumped. Had the wind snatched the woman from the balcony? Why had Tiffy thought she was still breathing? Is there a last exhalation, a final slackening when every muscle relaxes, when all the tension drains away from the body, when the organs stop working? When the heart stops beating?

In the following days and weeks, our clientele pieced together various details about the woman who'd died. She was under forty and Russian. She'd lived alone in a small apartment on the sixth floor, not in contact with anyone, not speaking to anyone. Many of them knew the woman by sight. She had often walked through the estate, limping, dragging a leg behind her.

'She'd already jumped once before,' Tiffy said. 'It hadn't worked. Probably not high enough. That's what did her leg in.'

Now it's May again. The doves are cooing, the hares are hopping, the wind is blowing. The diary is still jam-packed and Tiffy still isn't rich. People will soon be coming to pick the ripe cherries. When I stand in front of the salon and blink into the sun, I stay close to the wall. When I take the rubbish out, I steer clear of the spot by the manhole cover. I wave to the lesbian couple when they're walking their dogs on the grass.

FRAU FRENZEL

There are about eleven thousand dogs registered in the district of Marzahn-Hellersdorf. This makes it Berlin's top district for dogs, followed by Reinickendorf and Spandau. One of the eleven thousand is Amy. Amy is seven years old and belongs to Frau Frenzel. Frau Frenzel is one of my clients. I look after her feet every six weeks.

Frau Frenzel is seventy years old. She views the world with a cheerful contempt and won't let anything or anyone spoil her mood. She reminds me of a hedgehog, with her nose perkily pointing upwards, lively button eyes and a grey spiked mullet straight out of the 80s, neatly trimmed to one length on top and standing up like prickles, but longer around the ears and at the back. Whenever I see Frau Frenzel, I have to banish the thought that she might get her hair cut at the dog groomer's round the corner, which is just as popular as our beauty salon. Of course, it goes without saying that Frau Frenzel would never go to the dog groomer's for a trim, not even for Amy, as Amy, with whom Frau Frenzel shares her life, is a short-haired dachshund.

The footbath done, Frau Frenzel sits back in the chair and lets herself be pampered. I pluck embedded light brown dog hairs out of her soft, slightly slippery soles. Frau Frenzel tells me Amy moults a lot, despite her short coat. When Frau Frenzel lathers Amy up and rinses her off in the bath, the hairs she clears out afterwards fill the plughole strainer twice over. When it's Frau Frenzel's turn to shower, Amy won't leave her alone afterwards. She slobbers over Frau Frenzel's feet, ankles and calves with a devotion that is inexplicable to Frau Frenzel but delights her nonetheless. Every morning Amy wakes Frau Frenzel up by hopping onto her bed and licking her mistress, preferably her armpits. Then they're off for their first walk, which is followed by others spread throughout the day. In the evening, Amy and Frau Frenzel snuggle up on the sofa and watch a celebrity gossip programme on TV.

While I'm trimming her nails, Frau Frenzel asks me if I know Costa Cordalis.

'The singer,' I say, and sing one of the lines from his biggest hit.

'He had some fat taken from his bum and had it injected into his face,' Frau Frenzel says. 'When someone goes to give him a peck on the cheek, they're actually kissing his arse!'

Frau Frenzel smiles her smile of disdain; she distances herself from men, and not just the famous ones. She's done with men. She's laid two of them 'below ground'. She had two sons with the first, one of whom died in a car crash at the age of twenty-eight. Her second partner left behind an unbearable adopted daughter. At least he wasn't slow in kicking the bucket, which even years later Frau Frenzel is relieved about: 'Better ten dachshunds than one man.'

I push back her cuticles and in the folds of her left big toe I discover a dog hair that I remove with a certain sense of finder's pride. Frau Frenzel's feet don't need long with the nail drill and I don't have much hard skin to deal with either.

I pump a dollop of lime-scented skincare lotion into my hand. Frau Frenzel sits back, all set to enjoy her massage, and she tells me about the dachshund meet-up at the Lichtenrade Dachshund Ranch. It was meant to be the world's biggest ever dachshund meet-up. They were aiming for 666 dachshunds, which would have beaten the record of 601 dachshunds in one place by sixty-five, securing a place in *Guinness World Records*. Unfortunately, though, only 146 dachshunds turned up in Lichtenrade. All of Frau Frenzel's hedgehog face is lit up; the fact they didn't break the record doesn't really bother her at all.

I finish her massage and slip her socks onto her feet. She points to the window and exclaims, 'There they are, all three of them, come to pick me up!'

I turn around. Frau Ponesky is standing outside the window waving, despite the mirror coating that means she can't see a thing, and in her other hand she has two leads, attached to two dogs: Amy and Leila, a long-legged, lean mixed breed, whose fluffy black hair looks freshly groomed. Frau Ponesky, another of my clients and in her seventies, also looks freshly groomed. Of course, it goes without saying that she entrusts her dyed-black and artfully waved hair to the hands of someone who styles human hair.

Frau Frenzel pays and we step out of the salon into the warm late summer's day. A shared joy erupts. Amy is insanely happy to see her mistress again, wagging her pointy dachshund tail furiously, and Frau Frenzel is insanely happy to see her beloved Amy again. Leila, Frau Ponesky's mixed breed, is happy to see Frau Frenzel, Amy's mistress, again, and Frau Ponesky and Frau Frenzel are happy to see each other again. Over the course of many dog walks, they've become true, close and loyal friends through their love of dogs.

Frau Ponesky blurts out some news she's just read in a tabloid. Did we know that some celebrities – Julia Roberts, for example – smear haemorrhoid ointment on their faces, as it's meant to have some kind of firming effect? Frau Frenzel and I are in stitches over the thought of Julia Roberts slowly but surely freezing her facial expressions with haemorrhoid ointment, and we both agree we'll stick to our wrinkles.

I crouch down towards Amy. She has a dear little face – a black nose, a pale brown muzzle, shaggy brows overhanging shiny eyes edged by tiny lashes – and very short legs. She sniffs my wrists and I whisper, 'It's lime, I'm sorry.' Amy looks at me, a little shy, a little reproachful, and I think of something the philosopher Dr Grosse, another of my clients, once said to me as he sat in the chiropody chair: 'Of course animals can talk, but they choose not to.'

Frau Frenzel has attached a laminated tag, a tiny ID card, to Amy's collar: Amy Frenzel, date of birth, address, phone number, passport photo. Frau Ponesky and I say it's adorable, and Frau Frenzel reveals that soon Leila, Frau Ponesky's mixed breed, will be having a birthday and she's giving her one too.

The women let their dogs off the lead. Amy and Leila dash around on the grass in front of our salon. They nip at each other's heels and roll over. Leila jumps up into the air, making her black ears flap. Lower to the ground, Amy blasts off like a little light brown missile. Frau Ponesky, Frau Frenzel and I stand at the edge of the grass.

The women call to their dogs and we say goodbye. They walk off through the estate in a cosy foursome. Tall, thin Frau Ponesky striding ahead on the left, with the slender, black Leila on her lead. Hedgehog prickles bouncing as she moves, Frau Frenzel and Amy, the short-haired dachshund, patter along on the right.

Frau Ponesky has an appointment with me next Wednesday. Frau Frenzel will look after Frau Ponesky's mixed breed while she's at the salon. After Frau Ponesky's had her foot massage, Frau Frenzel, Amy and Leila will appear outside the salon's mirrored window, ready to pick up Frau Ponesky. Joy will erupt outside the salon. Leila will be insanely happy to see her mistress again, wagging her fluffy black tail furiously. Frau Ponesky will be insanely happy to see her beloved Leila again. Amy, Frau Frenzel's dachshund, will be happy to see Frau Ponesky, Leila's mistress, again, and Frau Frenzel and Frau Ponesky will be happy to see each other again. Then they'll let their dogs off the lead. Amy and Leila will go for a run around on the grass.

When I get home from work in the evening, I google 'Costa Cordalis now', see some grim photos and think of Amy's dear little face. Then I google 'dachshund life expectancy'. They have long lives, in comparison to other breeds – fifteen years if they're looked after well.

HERR HÜBNER

Most of my clients are regulars and pay me a visit every four to seven weeks. Over time, I've got to know these clients, their foibles and their quirks, their life stories, their fates. I'm fond of them, I know what they like, and I'm always pleased to see them again, safe and well, after a few weeks. With their frequent care, my regulars' feet are in good condition.

Every now and then, so-called walk-in customers show up, even though they can't walk very well: painful corns, ingrown nails or the acute consequences of a bloody self-experiment in the privacy of their own bathroom drive them to our salon. These walk-in customers also include out-of-towners, people with vouchers and people who only attach temporary importance to how their feet look (a spa break, a stay in hospital or a new girlfriend). Sometimes I manage to convert a walk-in customer to a regular, if the first appointment goes well.

Tiffy calls people who come to the salon for the first time newbies. When a newbie arrives at our salon, I place bets with myself: follow-up appointment? Tip? Apology? I always bet on the apology and I always win. It doesn't matter whether it's a construction site foreman or someone who fancies himself, tattooed from head to foot, whether it's a pregnant woman or an old one, whether they're academics or without two brain cells to rub together – in actual fact, everyone who takes their shoes and socks off in a chiropody room for the first time apologizes for their feet. It makes no difference what condition they're in. It's all new and unfamiliar; the contact is a little too intimate; it's embarrassing – all of this is reflected in the apology.

One Wednesday morning, I read the name 'Herr Hübner' in the diary.

'Do you know him?' I asked Tiffy.

She shook her head. 'Newbie,' she said, 'bit of a strange character. Came with his wife to make the appointment. I think she wears the trousers.'

At three o'clock, Herr Hübner was standing outside the door: a man in his late fifties, gone to seed, in a slouchy grey hoodie and baggy grey jogging bottoms. He was looking through the window with unmistakable reluctance. His wife was standing next to him, a plump woman dressed in black, with unkempt long hair dyed bright red. On Herr Hübner's other side stood a young girl, thin, pale, flat-faced, an unassuming creature only given shape by her eyes edged with black eyeliner, presumably Herr Hübner's daughter. When I opened the door and introduced myself, he didn't want to give me his hand and hid behind his wife. She and her daughter tried to coax him inside. When that didn't help, they gave him a shove over the threshold with their combined strength, while he acted the lame horse. Herr Hübner looked round the reception area in fear and then at me with his strangely watery eyes. I invited the family to take a seat while I prepared the footbath. When I returned, I explained that the treatment would last about an hour; the ladies were welcome to stay or they could go off and do some shopping. 'We'll stay,' said the mother; the daughter nodded. I asked Herr Hübner to follow me into the chiropody room. I was followed not only by him, but also by the women, in single file. I said I'd rather his entourage waited in the reception area, but neither I, nor the room's confined space, nor even the lack of chairs could drive the women away. They stood there, in the way, making it clear I should keep out of things I knew nothing about. I showed Herr Hübner to his place in the chiropody chair and he turned around completely before sitting down hesitantly, as if he was afraid of getting dirty. I moved the footbath into position and Herr Hübner took his shoes off, or rather kicked them off his feet. They were ancient Crocs with air holes, a faded black and worn out of shape. What came into view was something from the animal kingdom. I've blanked out the stench of it. I realized Herr Hübner's appendages would have ruined any socks in seconds and no closed shoe would have been able to house them. And so, for years on end, in summer and in winter, he'd gone round with his bare feet in these rubber-dinghy-shaped slippers. As Herr Hübner worked himself up to putting his feet in the water, he whimpered softly and turned his fearful puppy eyes to the women, who cajoled him again, reassuring and encouraging him to get through the difficult hour that lay ahead of him. I had the feeling that I wasn't so much his helper as his enemy. While I slipped on my latex gloves, something else occurred to me. Something was missing. The apology. Ironically, the very person whose feet had achieved an unrivalled level of neglect did not apologize. Not even his wife or his daughter offered an apology; they obviously didn't feel the need for any explanation about what I had to tend to. There they stood without a word, to the left and right of the chiropody chair, with Herr Hübner whimpering in the middle.

After I'd washed his feet, I examined the extent of the neglect more closely under the magnifying lamp.

'Your husband hasn't trimmed his toenails for a long time,' I said to the plump woman, as I liberally disinfected Herr Hübner's feet.

'He's not my husband!' replied the plump woman with an indignant laugh.

'So he's not your father, then?' I asked the flat-faced one.

'Nope,' she said, rolling her kohl-rimmed eyes.

I took my biggest clippers out of the cupboard. His nails – claws several centimetres long – could only be trimmed bit by bit. I needed the full strength of both my hands and had to stand up from my stool for greater leverage. Herr Hübner's whimpers became louder and he acted as if I was trying to take something valuable away from him. The plump woman patted his arm lovelessly and the flat-faced one made a cursory attempt to do the same. The plump woman said, 'It'll be over soon' and 'It's not that bad,' and the flat-faced one agreed. Meanwhile they glanced at his feet with wrinkled noses and a look of repulsion on their faces that they managed to hide from Herr Hübner but not from me. Their eyes told me that something must have gone badly wrong in my life for me to be forced to earn my money doing such repulsive and herculean work.

I'd cut away the worst and applied some callus softener, to make the crusts around his nail folds more supple. When I took a probe from the kidney bowl and started on them, Herr Hübner started a new bout of whimpering. I paused, let the probe drop and looked at the three of them. First at the flat-faced girl, who was chewing gum, then at the plump one, who was taking a peek at her watch, then at Herr Hübner. I fixed my gaze on him, peering questioningly into his puffy face, into his weepy eyes. I realized he couldn't be as old as he looked. A short silence ensued.

'My darlings,' Herr Hübner cried out in the silence, 'what would I do without you? Without you I'd never have made it here!' He turned right and left, grasped the hands of his two companions and pressed them to his chest. 'I don't know how to thank you! I just hope you like the cake I made especially for you!' The ladies withdrew their hands and patted Herr Hübner again: 'Yes, sure,' 'So kind of you,' 'We'll love it.'

I carried on with my work. I picked out no end of dead skin from his nail folds with the probe. I made more improvements with a finer one, then followed on with some clippers. I swept up the heap of nail clippings lying on the ground under Herr Hübner's feet. The three of them were chatting about the cake, but not without following what I was doing out of the corners of their eyes. By then I had the impression that even Herr Hübner was disgusted by what I was doing.

'Bye,' said the plump woman, out of the blue. 'Bye,' echoed the flat-faced one and, as if on cue, the women turned on their heels and left the room.

'See you tomorrow, my darlings!' Herr Hübner chirruped after them. 'Enjoy the cake!'

The salon door closed.

'Where are they going?' I asked in surprise. 'We haven't finished yet.'

'They've finished work,' Herr Hübner said, visibly relaxing. He made himself comfortable in the chair; it wouldn't have taken much for him to casually cross his legs. I looked at the clock: half past three, on the dot.

'Social workers,' said Herr Hübner. 'The thin one is the fat one's student.'

With the coarsest burr head and the highest setting I'd ever used, I set about the surface of his nails. Herr Hübner didn't complain or make a fuss; he didn't even notice me fitting a blade in the scalpel handle. While I shaved thick strips off his heels, he told me stories about his life, not without some pride. He had learned nothing at school and he'd never worked, but ever since his teenage days he'd drunk like a fish. He'd sat rotting in his *plattenbau* apartment and – once the path to his bed had become inaccessible from the sheer amount of rubbish – spent his nights in his armchair in front of the TV. When the rubbish started cascading over his balcony railing, the neighbours called the police and lodged a complaint. That's how Herr Hübner ended up in the hands of psychologists, therapists and social workers, vowed to improve himself and got a place in supported housing for addicts. 'Every so often I have to go to a self-help group and chunter on for a bit, and sometimes I have to go to the office to fill out forms, but apart from that they leave me in peace, to watch the telly, lie out in the sun or see mates.'

'And bake cakes,' I say.

Herr Hübner waved this aside. 'I wouldn't touch that cake myself. But the girls need something for their efforts, so I do my best.'

Meanwhile I had smoothed down his heels with my file, rubbed cream into his feet, brought the chiropody chair back down to earth and pushed in the leg rests. Herr Hübner slipped on his filthy Crocs and shuffled after me to the till, where I asked him for twenty-two euros.

'That's a bit steep!' he said, and winked at me. 'Ah well, it's no big deal. The state pays for it all, doesn't it?'

I felt courageous enough to ask Herr Hübner why one of his social workers couldn't cut his toenails. Or he could even do it himself. 'It's not in their contract. I can't expect my girlfriend to do it and I'm depressed,' he said, and he left the salon without rushing, without a thank you and without a goodbye.

ERWIN FRITZSCHE

Berlin's chaotic house-numbering system doesn't stop at Marzahn. The streets split off treelike into several branches through the estates. The road our salon is on has two separate lanes, one running behind the high-rises and one in front of them. It covers almost a mile but has only fifty-five street numbers, as it's interspersed with squares and green spaces. People unfamiliar with the area often wander over the grass in front of the salon in confusion, looking for the health centre at number 30. We're number 32, about two minutes on foot from the health centre. To get there, you have to choose between two circuitous routes that go past all kinds of things, but no number 31. And that's just one example.

At ten past two, there's an insistent banging on the salon door. I open it and let in a short, fat, agitated man – glasses, bald head, fabric tote bag, brightly checked shirt. He almost missed the place, he complains; he looked for the number but went in the wrong direction, and that's why he's so late.

My newbie isn't unfamiliar with the area. As he told me when he rang to make the appointment, he's been living in the neighbourhood for twenty years. He made his appointment eight weeks ago. When I asked him for his name and a contact number, he said, 'It's Erwin here. It's Erwin Fritzsche.' He asked me about seven times, 'So this foot business, you can actually do it, can you?' His mistrust amused me, but I was sure my newbie wouldn't show up. He'd probably have long since found another chiropodist, or just let it drop.

He's now sitting in front of me, with his trouser legs rolled up and his feet in water. He stumbles over his words, catches his breath and only calms down when I assure him that we'll have enough time and that, apart from his initial wild goose chase, it's all worked out fine in the end for both of us. He's even remembered the towel I mentioned eight weeks ago, which surprises me, earning Erwin Fritzsche some praise.

I dry off his solid and slightly knobbly feet, the sort I like to call 'potato feet'. As the obligatory apology for their condition, he explains that 'one of those chiropo-whatnots butchered my big toes, both of them. They went completely septic. I could hardly walk. They had to be lanced!'

Now I understand his mistrust on the phone. He was afraid of being mutilated again. When I send the throne up into the air and inspect his feet under the magnifying lamp, I can see two clean, fully healed incisions in the inner folds of his big toes.

'When did the chiropodist mess them up?' I ask.

'Four weeks ago,' says Erwin Fritzsche.

That can't possibly be right.

I can also see that his toenails have been cut, not beautifully, but functionally, each with three edges – snip snip snip. Two to four weeks ago, I'd guess, and I ask if he's trimmed them himself.

'No, I can't manage it. It was a friend of mine. She helps me out.'

The friend takes great care of him. He does have qualms about accepting her help though, as 'she's forty-eight, and I'm seventy-three. It's just wrong somehow.' Sure, he's always known women who have been keen to help him, mostly younger ones. He's done well with younger women all his life, although he's never been close to older ones (or even ones his own age). In rehab, for example, 'some old do-gooder' was always knocking on his door: 'She kept coming to fetch me for a game of cards.' But Erwin Fritzsche didn't want to play cards with old people; he preferred flirting with the young physiotherapist.

'What kind of rehab?' I ask.

'I had...' Erwin Fritzsche hesitates.

I look up from his toes to his face. His glasses make his eyes look bigger.

'I had a heart attack and I had a stroke too.'

His eyes tell me he has just about managed to remember these words, but that every trace of their meaning is gone. His eyes are full of wonder.

'I had all of that,' he continues, knowing only that it's a bad thing to have had all of that, and that nothing is ever the same as it was, once you've had all of that.

I don't ask him when he had all of that; I ask him about diabetes and blood thinners.

'Don't know. I take so many pills. I don't really get what the doctors tell me any more. Early stages of dementia, one told me.'

Such terrible words again. Erwin Fritzsche looks at me searchingly with his enlarged eyes, bewildered, embarrassed. He's on the verge of losing track. There are blind spots, and when he notices them, his coordinate system falters. His inner map crumples. Erwin Fritzsche's timeline does somersaults in his head.

That's why he was so agitated when he couldn't find the salon. That's why he thinks it was four weeks ago that a chiropodist butchered his big toes. That's why he has qualms about asking too much of his younger friend. As for the towel, he will have written himself a note, alongside today's appointment, maybe on a notepad positioned next to his phone especially for this purpose.

I can't help my newbie out of this impenetrable muddle. But I can round off the corners of his nails and lure him back to the dry land he knows.

'What do you do for a living, Herr Fritzsche?'

As a young man, Erwin Fritzsche went to the Friedrichstadt-Palast, 'the old theatre they knocked down, on Schiffbauerdamm, before they built the new one', and declared his intentions to the doorman. Once he was allowed in, he knocked on the director's door and asked for a job. The director took him on as a lighting apprentice. From then on, Erwin Fritzsche climbed up extremely tall ladders, installed spotlights on the ceiling, slid green, red, violet and yellow filters over the lamps and cast colourful, magical light over the stage. He raves about the director; he raves about the revues in the Friedrichstadt-Palast. And suddenly I see the brightly checked shirt he's wearing over his little round belly as a reminder of a good time, straight out of *Ein Kessel Buntes*, the old East German TV entertainment show that was often recorded in the Friedrichstadt-Palast.

Did he meet any famous people? Of course! Erwin Fritzsche saw them all up close: Dean Reed, Veronika Fischer, Michael Hansen and the Nancies. Even the foreign artists, like Zsuzsa Koncz, Jiří Korn, Bonnie Tyler, Boney M., Miriam Makeba, Milva. And Frank Schöbel – Erwin Fritzsche wouldn't hear a word against him, he was really nice. What about Helga Hahnemann? 'No! She was horrible. She thought she was a cut above. When she got it into her head that she wanted to rehearse, all the chorus girls had to leave the dance hall straight away.' His heart didn't belong to Helga Hahnemann, it belonged to the showgirls who made up the famous Friedrichstadt-Palast chorus line: long legs, long necks, long hair, and in between them, short, fat Erwin. He's the sort of guy women like because he treats them well. A guy lacking in physique or macho posturing; a dear, good-natured, trustworthy, fun and charming chap.

His heels smooth, his feet massaged and soft, Erwin Fritzsche is pleased – it hasn't hurt at all and they look good too. He'll show his smart feet to his friend tomorrow when she comes to see him again. 'There, you see, little Erwin, it's fine,' she might say, running a hand first over his spherical head, then over his spherical belly. That's what I'd do, anyway.

'You're a diamond,' he says.

I nod proudly and add myself to the line of younger women who help Erwin Fritzsche, threading myself onto the diamond necklace along with all the other diamonds Erwin Fritzsche has known over his lifetime.

After he's paid, he asks for another appointment, which I write down on a card for him. He spends a long time rummaging around in his wallet and finally reveals a large coin, which he gives to me. 'If you hold on to this, you'll never be out of pocket.' It is a coin from 1973, twenty East German marks, a special issue with the head of Otto Grotewohl.

He says goodbye at the salon door, looks around to get his bearings and turns right, fabric tote bag in hand. He falters in his stride, as does his coordinate system.

It would help if the street numbers in Marzahn were less chaotically arranged. If they were arranged like the famous Friedrichstadt-Palast line of girls, their sixty-four long womanly legs dancing, with Prussian precision, beguilingly uniform and always predictable: left kick, right kick, left kick, right kick… Will Erwin Fritzsche come back in six weeks? Will he find the salon? I'd say the odds are fifty-fifty.

THE NOLLS

Flocke and I are standing in front of the salon. We're having a cigarette while we wait for our next clients. Flocke is my colleague; she is a nail technician. Her hair is short, red and tousled, she wears a different pair of pretty earrings every day and she has a maternal roundness that brings out an urge for a cuddle in me.

Before she started working in our salon, Flocke worked in hospitality for decades, as a barmaid in the bars of Berlin. She has this previous life to thank for her deep, smoky voice. When Flocke's hips, knee and feet made it impossible for her to stand behind the bar for ten hours a day any more, she retrained for a job involving a chair. To start with, she had problems adapting to her new environment; on one occasion, when she had to repair a client's gel nail, she lost her temper: 'The fucking piece of shit won't stick!' The client fled, horrified.

Since then, Flocke has adapted her tone of voice to the service industry's client-centric ethos and recovered her aplomb behind the manicure table. Women sit before her peacefully purring, tamely holding out their little paws, filled with the same sense of well-being that the men used to feel on their stools at the bar, drinking from their beer glasses with their lips and from Flocke's cleavage with their eyes. Flocke listened then and listens now to all the stories with stoic patience, even when they're repeated for the twelfth time. She absorbs all the confessions like a sponge and keeps them to herself with consummate discretion. I like spending my breaks with Flocke. Being with her feels like home.

We stub out our cigarettes as the Nolls, mother and daughter, come tottering around the corner. Frau Noll Senior is bent over the walking frame she can barely push. Her jacket flaps around her tiny body, her too-long sleeves hang over her hands and the fabric of her creased trouser legs bunches up over her shoes. Old Frau Noll's clothes have become too big for her; she must weigh forty kilos at most. She is our oldest client at ninety-six, but could easily be ten years older.

Next to her, Frau Noll Junior waves and says hello, bares her teeth, rushes up to us, throws her arms around our necks and smothers us in kisses. In return, we show our pleasure as best we can. Old Frau Noll stands mute next to her daughter like a pet on a lead and doesn't even raise her head. We greet her with care and affection. Old Frau Noll smiles in a way that says it doesn't matter whether she's smiling or not.

Flocke holds the salon door open. Old Frau Noll tries to push her walking frame over the ledge but doesn't quite manage it. Her daughter grabs the handles and shoves it over the threshold. 'Get in there, then!'

Inside, I help Old Frau Noll out of her jacket. She's wearing a lime-green and mouse-grey blouse with gold buttons, her tiny crinkly neck protruding forlornly from her high collar. She's dressed up for the occasion. When I take her little beret off her head, I get a shock. There's a big dark red scab right on her fontanelle. Around it, her scalp is bare and a few remains of white hair stick out in all directions like baby hair.

'Frau Noll,' Flocke and I ask, 'what's happened to your head?'

'She tripped on the balcony step and landed on the clothes horse.' Frau Noll Junior holds her fist over her mother's mutilated little head, as if she was going to pick a bunch of carrot tops, and with two fingers – snip snip – she shows how she cut her mother's hair with the scissors. Old Frau Noll stands there like a lost vegetable puppet from a children's show.

Flocke helps her to the manicure table with her walking frame. I push the chair under her little body that no longer boasts a bottom, her little body with its back hunched between its narrow shoulders.

As I'm carrying the footbath through the reception area, her daughter inspects the salon. She stuffs a couple of business cards into her trouser pocket and nips to the water dispenser to fill herself a glass. She picks up the colour supplements laid out on a table, drops them and follows me, but not before she's fished two Ferrero chocolates from the glass bowl on the table.

In the chiropody room, she plonks herself onto the throne, takes her shoes and socks off and splashes her feet into the water. Her eyes are scouring the cream dispensers and tubes.

'You got anything new on offer?' She uses the informal 'you' with me, although she's never invited me to do the same with her; to this day I still don't know what Frau Noll Junior's first name is.

Her feet are dirty, although it's too late in the year for gardening. She maintains she washes her feet, but I know she's lying. In truth, she wants to give me plenty of work for the price she's paying. I do what needs to be done; every client gets the same treatment here. But with her, the entertainment programme switches off. I work silently, giving monosyllabic responses to her complaints about her wayward mother, the miserable malingerer who deliberately puts it on, who acts all weak and helpless but can see and hear much better than we all think.

In contrast to her mother, she hasn't dressed up. She's thrown on the same baggy sweater as always and as always she has no bra underneath. Noll Junior used to breed cattle. At some point, her shaggy hair was sloppily dyed blonde. There is a grey shimmer in her thatch and the wrinkles on her face are wrinkles of parsimony. At sixty-five, though, she still comes across as perky and youthful, around the same age as Flocke and me. I let her unwrap her squirrelled-away Ferreros on her own, in spite of the tremor plaguing her hands. I register her struggling, but I won't help her one bit. Then it's my turn to struggle: with her toenails, which are hopelessly ingrown. Under her distrustful gaze, I poke out reams of dead cuticle from her nail folds, and black stuff that's a combination of sock lint and something else.

Next door I can hear Flocke's deep voice in whisper mode: 'Has your nail split again?' Unfortunately, Noll Junior hears it too and roars through the wall that she's told her mother a thousand times not to use her fingernails to open up the meals on wheels lids but no, her mother doesn't listen, she'd always rather pick at things, especially the scabs that form on her sores. There isn't a peep from Old Frau Noll. Even Flocke falls silent. I keep quiet too.

I scrub around the thick, hard calluses under the balls of Noll Junior's feet until I'm sweating. After she has demanded and received another helping of WD cream, Flocke and I swap clients. Noll Junior goes for a manicure and Noll Senior comes for a pedicure.

When Flocke brings Old Frau Noll through to me, I cast a glance in her direction. Flocke and I can communicate without words and without our clients noticing a thing.

I sit Old Frau Noll on the throne, take her little shoes and socks off and roll up her much-too-long trousers. Flocke wraps her in a blanket, as she is always cold; I fetch a new footbath and show her little feet, two blue-and-red-marbled miniatures, the way into the water. I unwrap a Ferrero.

'Chocolate,' I whisper, stroking her cheek. Physical contact and voice are the best things to use when approaching someone whose field of vision reaches no further than a newborn's. Old Frau Noll emits a hoarse note of delight, snaps her little mouth open and, with a slurp and a smack, the Ferrero is gone. I dry off her feet, send the throne up in the air and pull the leg rests forward, but don't extend them – that's how small my client is. She sits completely still, her plucked head with the scabby wound hanging slightly forward, her eyes barely more than two small red-rimmed holes. She can sense everything I do and she doesn't want to disturb or miss a thing. Her hands on the blanket are still shiny from Flocke's massage; her nails have been filed into perfect ovals. Her fingers are slightly curled and bunched together; even her little thumbs sit close to her index fingers. Her hands remind me of the claws of a dead bird that has fallen out of its nest. I turn the drill on, and she lifts her little head and says, 'Buzzing.'

While her daughter lives in the village of Alt-Marzahn, in a house with a garden and a dog, Old Frau Noll is being battery-farmed in a neighbouring *plattenbau*; she isn't allowed to leave her one-room apartment alone, not even to go onto the balcony. Her daughter pops in every day, then locks her mother back in and keeps the key in her trouser pocket. For the rest of her life, Old Frau Noll sits there and waits. For death, for an end to total dependence and for her daughter, whose appearance she probably fears most. She no doubt picks at her skin to contribute towards her own dissolution.

The drill goes quiet. Next door I can hear Flocke talking to Noll Junior about carnivorous plants. At some point early on, Flocke made the mistake of being friendly and giving her a pitcher plant, like the one in Flocke's window, and carnivorous plants have been an obligatory topic of conversation ever since.

Since she is battery-farmed, Old Frau Noll's feet don't have any hard skin. I put the paddle away and venture a question. 'Frau Noll,' I say in a loud voice, with my face towards her so she can read my lips, 'what did you do for a living?'

She hesitates and even tenses up. She has unlearned how to talk, but she gives it her all at this moment.

'Industrial buyer,' she says, then her upper dentures, grown too big for her just like her clothes, fall out of place. She quickly snaps her little mouth shut in time to catch them.

There's a bark from the next room: 'She was at the Narva light bulb factory.' Unlike me, Old Frau Noll doesn't flinch; she simply sits there like a wind-up doll whose mechanism is wearing out.

I take her little left foot and steadily stroke from the base joints of her toes along her instep towards her ankle joints. Everything feels so delicate, so easily broken. I draw on what I've learned over the course of many massages: contact over a wide surface area gives more pleasure than a targeted touch. One hand must always remain on the foot to avoid the sensation of abandonment. A moderate tempo shows I'm not in a hurry. Suddenly, Old Frau Noll cries out in a high, reedy, cracking voice, 'Beautiful.' And again: 'Beautiful.' And once more: 'Beeeaaauuutiful!'

In the reception area, I help her with her jacket. Then it needs zipping up. Because of her poor sight, Old Frau Noll can't manage it. Her daughter, with her tremor, is no better. Flocke can't bend down because of her bad knee. I, though, can crouch down, put my glasses on and pull her zip up.

Old Frau Noll needs to pee, so she turns round with her walking frame and moves towards the loo. Noll Junior objects: 'But you've got your coat on now! You could have thought about it earlier!' I ask her to help her mother to the toilet.

'She can go on her own!'

Rather than helping her mother, she makes a start on the goodbye kisses, throwing her arms around Flocke's neck and mine alternately. We do our best, our attention firmly on our client-centric ethos.

Old Frau Noll comes back from the loo and thanks us, and we wish her goodbye and hope her head's better soon. Flocke holds the salon door open. Old Frau Noll struggles with her walking frame over the little ledge.

'Get out, then!' screams her daughter.

We watch the Nolls go. Noll Junior turns round, bares her teeth and waves to us. We wave back.

'Do you think she pockets the care allowance?' Flocke says, wiping Noll Junior's wet kiss off her cheek.

'How do you manage to do her nails with that tremor of hers?' I ask.

'By holding tight,' says Flocke.

Old Frau Noll in her too-big clothes is plugging away with her frame; from behind, her back is all hump. Buzzing; industrial buyer; beeaaauutiful. That was the extent of my conversation with Old Frau Noll.

Back in the salon, Flocke disinfects the manicure table. I carry my footbath to the toilet. When I go to tip it out, I can see the loo is blocked. The water has come right up to the rim. Old Frau Noll must have had a mishap. I call Flocke. Flocke takes a look at the problem, goes to the kitchen, comes back with a huge rubber glove, pulls it on up to her elbow and delves deep into the toilet. She fishes out a large nappy liner and disposes of it in a bin bag. The water drains away.

'Wow, Flocke,' I say, dropping my head to her shoulder for a second, 'you're a hero.'

Flocke pulls the glove off. 'Cigarette?'

We stand outside. I light up. Flocke exhales her smoke and looks up at the tower block, her earrings sparkling. She starts talking.

She cleaned the toilets thousands of times in her bartending days, of course. Always after the bar had shut, but with certain customers she also preferred to check right away, armed with cleaning products and room spray so the loo could be used again. Flocke had seen it all: walls covered in shit, bins full of piss, vomit all over the washbasins. Once, she fished out some dentures with her rubber gloves, another time a glass eye, neither ever to be reclaimed. Over the years, a regular with a wooden leg had split several toilet seats. How or why remains a mystery. Some people who had missed their aim would repentantly push a banknote over the bar to Flocke for the cleaning. The worst, Flocke says, were the ones who left behind a pigsty and just disappeared without a word. They were often the flashier ones who talked all the talk at the bar, but whose tips were small or non-existent. Others who had nothing would still give her something, help her change a barrel or take drinks up the steep stairs for her, empty the ashtrays every so often, tidy away the garden furniture and put the chairs on the tables at the end of the night. Hard physical labour for a schnapps on the house. Those were the ones Flocke liked: those poor saps who behaved like gentlemen because the bar was their home, because Flocke was a mother to them and because they wanted to come back the next day and the day after that.

The phone rings. Flocke stubs her cigarette out and darts indoors. Through the window I can see how she smiles when she mentions the salon's name and her own, and although I can't hear her, I know she's taken her deep, smoky voice considerably higher, in line with her client-centric ethos. With the receiver at her ear, she disappears from my line of vision to the till area, where the diary is kept.

Sanitizing and decorating: I think I understand why Flocke is so big on these two things. Flocke likes it clean; Flocke likes it pretty. She decorates her apartment, our salon and even herself. She decorates her clients' nails, and while these colourful, glittery works of art could be seen as overdone and kitsch, maybe sometimes all the beauty in the world can be condensed into one single fingernail.

FRITZ

In Marzahn there is one attraction that draws in around fifteen hundred visitors a year: the Skywalk, a special construction made of metal.

From the ground floor of the tower block at 40–42 Raoul-Wallenberg-Strasse, you can take the lift to the twenty-first storey, climb some stairs, emerge at the top of the massive high-rise, scale some free-floating metal-grid stairs to reach windy altitudes and look down beyond your feet to the ground below. Having a good head for heights is an advantage. Once you're right at the top you get to a viewing platform. From seventy metres up, you have a magnificent view over Marzahner Promenade, over the rows of high-rises amid a froth of treetops, over the entire city as far as the TV Tower, as far as Lake Müggelsee and as far as Schönefeld Airport. Under the heavens, the clouds scud by and the expanses of Brandenburg stretch out before you.

Here, in this tower block, is where Fritz lives.

When Fritz first came to our salon, he was sixty-five years old and newly retired. I was forty-five and had started working as a chiropodist just a few months earlier. Fritz came because his wife had sent him. He was wearing jeans and trainers, and looked younger, certainly not like a pensioner. He was shy and charming, he smelled good and he apologized wholeheartedly and earnestly for his feet. Fritz thought they were an unreasonable imposition. He was expecting to be promptly sent back home because of them. I fell in love with them straight away.

Fritz's feet are well proportioned, with an almost classical beauty: sturdy ankles, round, firm heels, his insteps elegantly curved. Under his skin, which remains lightly tanned even in winter, his metatarsal tendons stretch out over his wide forefeet and into his muscular toes. Feet that offer an assured step. Feet with a dormant power. Sound, presentable feet.

However, his nails had thickened; some of them were the deep yellow of soaked lentils, others had brittle white layers and they were ragged from dryness. During my training I'd learned that these are called ram's horn nails. Although he could reach them, Fritz had been unable to cope with his toenails for some time; the tools he had at home weren't up to the job.

Fritz had got his thickened, porous nails from wearing heavy, clumpy work boots with steel toecaps. He was a skilled plastics technician. In GDR times, he had worked in Lichtenberg in a factory producing fishing line, planters and eggcups. After the Wall came down, when Fritz got the feeling his factory might be about to shut down, he wandered around West Berlin until he discovered a company that manufactured plastic granules; he sent in an application and was taken on. He spent the second half of his working life there in Reinickendorf, in work boots and protective clothing, with ear defenders and a face shield. The granule components were sent down enormous tubes and pipes to the production room, where they were heated to 130 degrees Celsius and mixed in a machine. It was hot, it was loud, the production processes were unforgiving and the workers had to yell to hear one another. One tiny error and the granules would fuse together in seconds and set into a rock-hard mass of plastic for eternity. It would take more than an eight-hour shift to break up the cooled mass with a pneumatic drill and remove it from the bottom of the machine.

At first I was wary of his nails, as I didn't have much experience. The better I came to know Fritz and his feet, the bolder I became. I'd put a coarser burr in the drill, select a higher speed. I would cut and sand and file, a little ambition taking hold of me. Fritz wasn't squeamish. He patiently let me experiment and we would joke together as I ground his nails thinner. When he left, he would always give me a generous tip and sometimes steal a kiss on the hand. Over the course of many sessions, Fritz's feet regained all their beauty once more. I secretly thought of them as my final-year project.

One day Fritz brought in a yellowed 1973 newspaper cutting from home. The grainy black-and-white photo showed a muscle-bound man with a solid stance, arms extended, head nestled in his huge neck. He was balancing a long rod on his forehead. High up, at the other end of the rod, a dainty, extremely flexible woman was doing the splits in a skintight sparkly costume. Fritz's parents – the bull neck and the sylph. Fritz comes from a family of artistes. His father travelled around with a circus all his life, training every day and fine-tuning his balancing act. He had his perch pole (the rod with the forehead attachment) custom-built, a special construction made of metal. Fritz's father had to replace the acrobatic woman at the upper end of his rod several times in his life; Fritz's mother was substituted by another woman at some point, and later on, his father performed the perch pole act with his own daughter, Fritz's sister. His father was still in the circus ring long after he'd turned seventy; he glowed with health and lived to ninety. Because of his parents' antics, Fritz was mainly brought up by his grandma, who suggested he learn a proper profession.

I had a vision of Fritz as a child standing behind the curtain in the big top, watching his parents. His father balancing the rod, his body taut with sheer tension and his eyes fixed on the woman in the air. His mother at dizzying heights, contorting her body with the utmost concentration – a sight for sore eyes, graceful and inaccessible.

Fritz told me stories about his parents' travelling circus, about his childhood with his grandma and about his shift work at the chemical plant. When I reached for the hard skin paddle, he grinned and tensed up. Fritz is ticklish in certain places that probably only I am aware of. I rubbed his heels smooth, grinned back and asked if I should stop. 'I don't mind being tortured by such a beautiful woman,' Fritz said softly. I took my time with the foot massage. Closed the door, dimmed the light and, for once, took my latex gloves off. I touched those beautiful feet, felt their warm skin, lowered my gaze. My hands contemplated their classical form. I took as long as I could with everything, every new movement, massaging slowly, surrendering myself. I sensed Fritz's gaze on me and heard myself breathing. With Fritz, silence is comfortable – an active and equivocal silence.

With a heavy heart, I let go of his feet. Then I looked up into Fritz's mellowed, mischievous face and his dreamy eyes. 'Ah,' Fritz sighed. 'If only I were twenty years younger.' I smiled, saying nothing but thinking something.

Fritz did not follow in his father's footsteps. No perch pole, no rod acrobatics. Fritz learned a proper profession. He has a wife, children and grandchildren; he has a little weekend garden plot out of town and a dog. He takes his dog for walks for several hours a day. Fritz is fit. Maybe he inherited his father's ruddy health. Maybe he also inherited his beautiful feet, with their assured step, from his father. Recently, when his son got married, Fritz was amazed he didn't need to buy a new suit: the one that had hung in his wardrobe unworn for twenty years still fitted him like a glove. I would have liked to see Fritz in his suit, although preferably barefoot.

The little weekend garden plot, the family gatherings, the grandchildren, the dog – they don't take up all of Fritz's time. That's why he also likes coming to see me. His chiropody appointment is the high point of his day. Since Fritz stopped working, boredom has been his greatest enemy.

To keep it at bay, Fritz runs up the stairs of the tower block at 40–42 Raoul-Wallenberg-Strasse once a day: hundreds of steps, from the ground floor up to the fifteenth storey where he lives. And although Fritz runs upstairs on a daily basis, he's never been to the top, to the twenty-first floor, not once. For Fritz, the Skywalk is like the perch pole. Fritz has on his roof what his father had on his forehead – a custom-built special construction made of metal.

WORK OUTING

The last day of November, a cold, drizzly Friday. Months ago Tiffy, Flocke and I marked it off and kept it free. The salon's closed, no clients today. We've bought a group train ticket and we'll be departing from the Ostbahnhof at 8.34. I can walk to the Ostbahnhof in twenty minutes; Tiffy and Flocke are coming from Marzahn S-Bahn station.

When I reach the concourse, I spot Tiffy standing in front of one of the cafés, rucksack by her side, shoulders hunched, hands buried in her pockets. A little cropped red coat, black harem pants, flat shoes.

'Where's Flocke?' I ask.

'Overslept,' says Tiffy.

We buy coffee and croissants and wander up to Platform One. We stand there munching and sipping. Tiffy's annoyed with Flocke. Flocke is often late, even to work.

'What's going on with Flocke?' she asks.

'She's getting old,' I say.

Tiffy looks at me as if it's the most stupid excuse she's ever heard. She looks down, happier to be talking to a station pigeon picking at our croissant crumbs, which raises her spirits. Tiffy is crazy about animals, about almost any animal, and when she shifts her attention to an animal, it always seems a little as though she's escaping from people. Having said that, it has to be animals with no more than four legs, as Tiffy regularly points out. She has a genuine spider phobia.

Flocke, on two legs, comes puffing up the stairs and rolls her eyes: she only woke up at ten to seven and shot out of bed, flung open the doors as if she were possessed, stuffed her clothes into her rucksack and didn't even manage to do her hair. So that's why she's wearing that dark blue hat with the rhinestones and the big bobble.

The local train arrives and we trundle off to Fürstenwalde, where we need to change trains after a half-hour wait. We go over the footbridge to reach the other platform. Stairs are Flocke's idea of hell, especially going up. She struggles up them, with one hand on the banister. I can't imagine what kind of painkillers Flocke has to knock back to get through days like these.

I need to go to the loo and so does Tiffy. There isn't one here. Flocke waits on the platform, while Tiffy and I go back up the stairs, back down the other side, look for a WC sign, ask in the station hall and then head off to the bakery café opposite, where there's a queue for the loo. They're charging everyone forty cents, as they have a monopoly on loos here. The key to the loo, which is passed from one person to the next in silence, has a nutmeg grater hanging from it, for some obscure reason. With everything so thin on the ground in Fürstenwalde – the number of loos, the train times, cultural offerings, population density – not even a dog would want to be buried here.

The little Niederbarnim train arrives promptly and takes just twelve minutes to reach Bad Saarow. We've perked up so much that a little excitement starts to kick in and we ask a plump young woman for a photo. She takes a picture of us on Flocke's phone.

Once we've arrived in the sleepy spa town, we walk from the station to Café Dreissig, a tradition we all agree we never want to change. A big breakfast, including scrambled eggs. It's busy, and Flocke isn't the only one to keep her hat on in here.

Our conversation reveals that Tiffy and Flocke played handball in their youth, while I used to do athletics and folk dancing. After twenty-seven years, Tiffy's taken up handball again and joined the SV BVB 49 club's second women's team in the Lichtenberg district, and she's generally always been sporty. She still forces herself out for a jog sometimes and she runs around Marzahn on Sundays. She also goes to dance classes with her partner. Whenever I can, I go to a fitness studio twice a week, preferably for step aerobics. Flocke has done nothing sporty since her schooldays, or at least nothing conventionally sporty. So from a sports point of view, Tiffy and I are in the majority.

We throw our coats on, grab our bags and walk to the Saarow thermal baths. Flocke and I smoke another cigarette. Tiffy doesn't smoke; she says it's pointless, unhealthy and much too expensive. She is absolutely right. But all the same, there are times when she has to join us outside the salon in the cold, if there's something we need to discuss. So from a smoking point of view, Flocke and I are in the majority.

We buy three day passes at the reception desk. Tiffy trudges up to the turnstile, holds her chip against the sensor and slips through. I go next and Flocke follows. We look for our lockers in the catacomb-like changing area and disappear into the cubicles, reappearing in our flip-flops and robes – Tiffy in deep purple, Flocke in white and me pale blue. We shuffle off to the showers. Then we can set foot in the thermal spa. It's not too busy. Plastic loungers, like rows of teeth, line the edges of the enormous pool radiating its soothing warmth beneath the tall colonnades. A tropical, saline climate. This is our third time here. It's all just as it always is, and now that we've shed our robes and towels and parked our flip-flops with the others at the pool's edge, gone barefoot down the steps into the water and gently slid in, we break into grins. It feels wonderful to immerse ourselves in this warm broth, freed from the need to bear our own weight. We float along sedately in the velvety water like manatees. We wouldn't change a thing, nothing for the better, nothing for the worse – all we want is to visit these thermal baths again and again. We paddle over to the little round Jacuzzi, then off to the bubble jets at the pool's edge and wait for them to turn on. We purr with pleasure as they increase their pressure and massage our tired lumbar vertebrae, our necks and behind our knees. That very first moment, long before our bodies grow accustomed to it, always knocks us out: that moment when the memory of the pleasure of it comes flooding back to us.

We paddle through the heavy translucent plastic curtains to reach the outdoor pools, emerging abruptly into ice-cold, clear air. Mist billows over the water's surface, gliding eerily and majestically past the Brandenburg pensioners' heads. A few unkempt pines rise into the pale grey sky. Tiffy, Flocke and I splash around. We hog every water feature, one by one. First the wide spout which sends water crashing over our tight necks. Then the frothy white geyser, whose centre we try our hardest to reach, though we never quite manage to. Then the mushroom. The mushroom is our favourite. If we're pulled into its whirlpool, we get spun around at breakneck speed, round and around the mushroom's stalk. It's a great laugh. As she flies past me, Flocke cries out, 'Watch you don't get caught speeding!' The whirlpool stops whirling and a waterfall shoots out of the mushroom's cap onto our heads; we have to hold on to withstand the force. By now we look like drowned rats, our hair ruined, sopping and dripping. Tiffy throws back what's left of her black bob and it sticks out in two fat tails over her ears. Flocke's short red hair is clinging to her head like a swimming cap. Time for the truth, embellishments null and void. To hell with keeping up appearances. I love it.

Flocke fights her way out of the mushroom's vortex – she probably wants to catch her breath at the poolside. I swim after her. I can see the red ball of her head, followed by a stretch of nothing, then the soles of her feet. Because of her hips, Flocke can't, or won't, do frog kicks, so she lets her feet simply hang behind her and their buoyancy keeps them just above the water's surface, wide, flat, turned inwards a little. Flocke is fifty-eight and she's spent her whole life on those soles. A life behind the bar, a life of standing, a life of walking. She'd wanted to be a barmaid for as long as she could remember. Her mother, who still lives in Rostock, wanted Flocke to train for a respectable job. At first, she tried working in the fish-processing plant in Sassnitz, sorting fish fillets on the conveyor belt for eight hours a day. She quit. She hitchhiked to Berlin with a friend and squatted in an empty house in Pflugstrasse, one of the few to be privately owned in the deepest of GDR times. She did an apprenticeship at Narva, became a machine operator and a team leader, the first woman to hold that position. Surrounded by young men and their cocky banter, Flocke learned to give as good as she got: sound preparation for her future behind a bar.

Although she had no training, she made enquiries at a restaurant. The man in charge said, 'We've got a booking tomorrow for forty knuckles of pork,' and he and Flocke practised carrying plates laden with cabbages, two on each arm. When the cabbages stopped rolling off the plates, he said, 'You've got the job.' That was Flocke's first forty knuckles of pork.

When she was twenty, Flocke went back home to her mother's in Rostock, because she was pregnant. Around the time Johnny was born, his father died of stomach cancer, at twenty-eight. Flocke doesn't make a big thing of it when she mentions it. I don't know how much she loved him. Back in Berlin, Flocke raised Johnny and worked in all the restaurants and pubs she could. Always shift work, often weekends. After the Wall came down, she became a landlady and took over a little pub in Lichterfelde. She kept it on for five years before giving it up and going back to being an employee. At the end of the 90s, when Johnny was a teenager, Flocke's phone would sometimes ring on a Friday. It would be Johnny and his group of friends. 'Get dressed,' they'd say, 'we'll pick you up in ten minutes,' and they'd hang up quickly, before Flocke could say no. From Friday to Sunday, Flocke would go to the Berlin techno clubs with her son and his mates. Every now and then she'd dance her way through two whole days without any sleep, and then bravely report for her shift at the pub on the Monday. Techno was Flocke's sport and it was maybe at this time that her osteoarthritis first set in.

Her techno time is over now. Johnny is thirty-eight, with a family of his own, and he delivers parcels for a logistics company. He doesn't often visit us at the salon. When he does, it's late, when we're about to close. He always looks tired and always brings a bottle of sparkling wine for us and a beer for himself. Flocke does her son's feet, I sit in the chair by the window and we talk. Johnny is a lovely man and I like being in his company, partly because of his deep, calm, warm voice. I can feel how close Flocke and Johnny are. And even today, when Flocke's phone rings it plays a Paul Kalkbrenner techno track.

Can you remember your midlife crisis – the fuzzy years, when you were turning around, at a loss, flagging from the tedium of swimming? Can you remember the fear of sinking in the middle of the big lake without a sound and without a cause – when you could see no land anywhere, no coastline, no shore, when you dropped to the bottom?

You've got Tiffy to thank for the fact that you're now swimming here in the Saarow baths. You first met her in

2010 – the year your last book came out. She was working as an instructor in a women's fitness studio. You'd do the moves she told you to do, and you liked the way she did them too, and the way she encouraged you; you liked her deep brown eyes, her fine-featured face, her cheeky laugh, and the way she threw her shaggy ponytail back. Her Saxon dialect made you feel at home and reminded you of your roots. Tiffy was a bundle of energy, five foot two with short, muscular legs. At that time she was in her mid-forties, the midpoint of her life, in the middle of her beautician's course. You were there when she offered her first treatments in the back room of the women's fitness studio to get some practice, and you watched her changing course again, with three children and a good twenty-five years of work behind her. Tiffy gave up being an instructor when she opened her beauty salon in Marzahn. You followed her and remained her client. When she turned fifty, she cut off her shaggy ponytail and got the black undercut bob she's had ever since. In early 2015 you took your usual trip to Marzahn for the full works, and you told Tiffy about your novella being turned down, about your daughter going to England for a year and about the cancer therapies prolonging the life of your partner, which had brought you both low. Tiffy did the right thing: she listened, said little, always lent an ear. While she was kneading your back with firm hands, you said, through the hole in the massage table where your face was resting, that something had to change, that you couldn't bear listening to yourself moaning any longer. You looked through the hole at Tiffy's feet as she said, 'Come and be a chiropodist here with me.'

She gave you the name of the school in Charlottenburg. At home, online, you saw the next course was starting in ten days. You talked it over with your partner and you signed up.

Flocke and I are chilling in front of a jet at the pool's edge. Tiffy appears in her black swimsuit, calling for us to go to the freshwater pool with her. Flocke won't move: she's going to stay where she is and carry on chilling; she says it's so nice that nothing hurts, just for once. Tiffy shrugs, calls us lazy cows and scuttles away in her flip-flops with the short, quick steps she takes at the salon when she's bustling around doing a thousand things at once. Tiffy is only four years younger than Flocke, yet seems much more dynamic. Both of them are ageing in interesting, very different ways. I am the youngest at forty-eight and I don't like to be outdone, or to be called a wimp. I climb an aluminium ladder out of the warm water, shiver in the Brandenburg November lunchtime cold, run over the wet tiles and clamber into the freshwater pool. I swim after Tiffy. We swim lengths, short lengths but plenty of them. We could be bouncing around like seahorses, as our feet can reach the bottom, but we swim. Breaststroke is fine, backstroke is tiring; we haven't mastered any other strokes.

Tiffy also has a son. He's twenty-one, the same age as my daughter, and he has a girlfriend. Tiffy's love for her son is so great she has to hide it a little; it's that same profound, vulnerable affection she wears on her sleeve for animals. Tiffy's son came later in her life, the baby of her family. She still lives with, and goes to her dance classes with, his father, who's ten years younger than Tiffy. She has two daughters from a previous relationship, both in their mid-thirties and with daughters themselves. Tiffy is a grandmother, albeit a non-practising one. The salon makes it impossible – she simply has no time. And in spite of the menopause, any grandmotherly feelings she might have are sidelined. She doesn't want to let herself go; she needs to stay fit and healthy for work. Tiffy is a workhorse. She has qualifications in sales management and a career at Kaufland hypermarkets behind her; after reunification she started working on the checkout at a branch in her hometown in the Erzgebirge Mountains, where she progressed to deputy manager. In 2003 she moved to Berlin with her family and managed the confectionery section of a Kaufland branch in Neukölln for seven years. When she talks about it now, she's still proud that her section looked immaculate – not a speck of dust, the shelves always freshly stocked, not a single bar past its best-before date. When, haggard from work and two slipped discs later, Tiffy handed in her notice and asked for compensation, her naive request was turned down with derision. Maybe her conviction that life is a losing game stems from that time. Tiffy never wants to ask for anything ever again. She wants to manage everything by herself. She doesn't expect thanks, but she doesn't want to have to thank anyone either.

Tiffy took out loans for her training course. She started small, in that windowless back room in the Friedrichshain women's fitness studio, then rented the salon in Marzahn, and in spite of the distance, other Friedrichshain clients and I followed her, because Tiffy was good, thorough and affordable, because she had a direct way of talking and strong, warm hands and because she always gave more than she received. Her salon took off and her clientele grew. Tiffy was her own boss; she worked hard and paid her bills. In place of exploitation came self-exploitation, a fashionable word Tiffy never uses, because she hasn't heard of it.

She's never crossed the threshold of any Kaufland again on principle, and once she triumphantly worked out with me how much money Kaufland had lost because she hadn't shopped there for almost ten years. She takes her personal revenge on the shitty shop that could have broken her. Tiffy's new, even mightier, enemy is the tax office, demanding extortionate amounts every quarter. She hangs in there, grits her teeth and lives so frugally that it pains Flocke and me sometimes. Every autumn the heating game commences, a battle that is waged without words – Flocke and I turn the heating up, Tiffy turns the heating down. So it sometimes comes to pass that Tiffy even sees us, her allies, as enemies. She makes the lion's share of the salon's turnover, she is tougher than anyone and she deserves a medal, but, like every medal, it has two sides: sometimes Tiffy suddenly bursts into tears and simply cries her eyes out. Flocke and I have learned to ignore this; it's the best thing we can do for her at those times.

Now Tiffy laughs, saying twenty-five minutes of exercise will do. We go and look for Flocke, who is resting with her arms outstretched on the edge of a round Jacuzzi. We join her in the lovely, bubbling, steaming warmth. We feel like chickens in a stockpot. We lift our feet out of the water and gaze at them happily: six of them, all of them presentable, because we look after each other's feet at the salon after closing time. Mine are the only ones with painted toenails; Flocke tried out a purple, which I don't mind – I'm happy to be Flocke's guinea pig. Apart from that I'm the least adorned of all of us – no colour in my hair, never any make-up, short fingernails. In my natural state, I call it. Because of her job, Flocke always has sparkling, colourful, thick, claw-like fingernails that look like weapons. Tiffy carefully makes herself up every morning at the salon before it opens; she owes it to her clients.

The bubbles massage our kidneys, giving us the urge to pee. It's also high time for a rewarding drink. We slip on our bathrobes and shuffle first to the loo, then to the lift, like a female version of the Olsen Gang in those old Danish films – Tiffy first, me in the middle and Flocke bringing up the rear – and arrive one floor up, in the same order, which seems to be our natural arrangement. We go into the restaurant, where we choose a table with a view over the baths. Tiffy orders three Aperol Spritzes, and we remember that the service here is abysmal, for one simple reason: whatever visitors consume here is recorded on the chip they wear on their wrists and they only get the bill at the end, and because spa visitors don't carry any change the waiting staff never get a tip. We know the meaning of tips.

We chat about our worst clients, about our favourite clients and about the weirdest, Frau Herrmann, Frau Boethelt and Frau Höhne-Butzlaff. The other day Frau Müller, who comes to me for her feet, booked an appointment with Flocke for a luxury manicure. Oh, Hannelore Müller? No, not Hannelore; no, not Ute Müller either, she only has treatments with Tiffy; yes, that's it, Regina Müller, the one who was being bullied at the pension insurance company where she worked, the one who's had nail fungus for twenty years.

Tiffy drinks like she works – swiftly. We manage to keep up with her. Flocke, though, with her bar experience, says the Aperol Spritzes we're knocking back are just 'child's play'. If that's the case, I'm happy to order a second round, especially as it's starting to get dark. I raise a glass to our children, who have all become great people, to our partners, with whom life is bearable at least, and to the considerable number of new clients who flood into our salon every month. As we're gabbling on, and as the sun goes down over Saarow baths, I am overcome with love, and I start eulogizing about the three of us, how we may have our quirks but we all have our hearts in the right place, how we all stick together when it matters and how we all do great work in a great salon with great clients, everyday heroines, that's what we are, especially Tiffy... who looks at me as if I'm not quite right in the head. She thinks I'm taking the piss, waves dismissively, cruelly cutting off my drivel. Flocke signals for a third round of Aperol Spritzes, while I launch into an ode to Marzahn and its inhabitants, who moved there forty years ago, now bravely coming to the end of their lives with their walking frames, their oxygen cylinders and their state pensions, sometimes spending whole days without speaking to another soul, pouring out their famished hearts to us when they come to the salon, gratefully absorbing every touch, happy for once not to be treated like imbeciles in the place that Tiffy, our dear little Tiffy, has built all on her own. Tiffy stares at me with her deep brown eyes welling up, then she loses the fight against her tears of emotion when I cry out, 'Our work is priceless! Our clients are the best! Marzahn, mon amour!'

'Oh God, the writer in her's coming out!' says Flocke, grinning.

'And so it must, honeybunch,' I say. 'Man shall not live by feet alone.'

'At least she's not using complicated sentences,' sobs Tiffy in her Saxon accent. She blows her nose as the lights come on in the Saarow baths. Candles flicker everywhere, their cosy light reflecting a thousand times over on the water, shimmering, glittering and sparkling. Ornamental lights hang in magical arrangements from the spa's heavens, sending out festive rays, and a solitary guitar can be heard, its notes gently bubbling up one by one into the light, poignantly, softly, beautifully.

Back in the catacomb-like changing area, we stand in front of the mirror, blow-drying our hair, red-eyed, thirsty, the skin on our faces parched: just like that feeling after swimming lessons at school. We trudge to the station, our rucksacks heavy with wet towels. The trains have stopped running. A cigarette with Flocke, waiting for the bus in the drizzle. After half an hour it creeps round the corner and we get on, along with a few lost souls. In the dark Tiffy looks out at the Brandenburg country roads. 'I haven't been on a bus for years.'

Change at Fürstenwalde. No loo; the bakery's closed, so we cross our legs and freeze on Platform Two until the local train arrives.

FRAU JANUSCH

My clientele consists mostly of pensioners. If I were a sociologist, I would divide their hobbies into three categories: dogs, gardening and minibreaks. I often see combinations of dogs plus gardening or gardening plus minibreaks. Minibreaks plus dogs is very rare. Hobbies are a hangover from a time when the pensioners were young, working and bringing up children. Hobbies are nurtured more and intensify at retirement age, but at some point the time always comes for the last dog, the last minibreak or the last summer in the garden.

Frau Janusch is in the gardening plus minibreaks category. When I first met her, she had a short pink hairstyle and a blue leather jacket. She was striking with her extravagant style. She would stroll up to the salon and lift her head to gaze at a magpie in a tree's branches, or to blink into the sun. If she'd nipped to the shopping centre before her chiropody appointment, she would happily show me what she'd bought – a little something to wear, some expensive leather shoes. We used to laugh about how Frau Janusch's pink hair went so wonderfully with my pink throne.

When I first bowed down before her, washing her feet, she told me about her husband, who depended on oxygen day and night and was no longer able to leave their apartment. I looked up, concerned for her, but before I could say anything, Frau Janusch made her pronouncement – one that I adhered to from then on: 'No sympathy!'

Jutta Janusch was born in 1942, a child of Berlin's Prenzlauer Berg district. She first lived with her parents in Pasteurstrasse, before moving to Käthe-Niederkirchner-Strasse, then called Lippehner Strasse. When she left school, she did a tailoring apprenticeship and specialized in leather. She soon landed a job with VEB Perfekt, a factory producing handbags, purses and leather clothing, in Heinrich-Roller-Strasse. She met her husband, Peter Janusch, born 1943, on the dance floor. He had just finished his apprenticeship with the furniture makers VEB Aufstieg, in Friedrichshain, and was serving in the army for eighteen months. Every weekend, Jutta and Peter would sashay around the Berlin dance halls: Behrens Casino, Clärchens Ballhaus, Bar Lolott. 'We'd get a bottle of Tokay and sip it very slowly to make it last all evening.' Their first apartment together was in Gaudystrasse: 'One room. Ground floor. There were ants all over the windowsill.'

Jutta Janusch was pregnant at twenty-three and had a daughter in 1965. In 1967 she and Peter got married and moved to Immanuelkirchstrasse, two rooms in the side wing of an apartment building, fourth floor, a stove for heating and an outside toilet. In the wedding photo she showed me, she's wearing winkle-pickers with stiletto heels. Her wedding dress reaches just below her knees, with a slender waist. A beautiful bride. Next to her is Peter, with a moustache, in a narrow-cut dark suit and tie: tasteful, laid-back. A hint of the West.

Peter Janusch passed the exam to become a master craftsman, left VEB Aufstieg and opened his own furniture workshop near Prenzlauer Promenade. Two storeys, twelve employees. Peter Janusch's furniture workshop made interiors for restaurants, restored furniture and mass-produced the chipboard surround for a radio cassette recorder made by VEB RFT Stern-Radio Berlin. The order book looked good. When they were very busy, Frau Janusch would help out at her husband's workshop in the evenings. But she always remained with VEB Perfekt, independent of her husband, which turned out to be a godsend, with her health insurance and pension.

At the end of the 70s they got themselves a garden plot out of town in Pankow-Heinersdorf with a little stone house, acquired in a roundabout way from a relative who'd gone to the West in 1961. Around that time Peter Janusch also began to take an interest in painting, and he went to evening classes at an art school. He would spruce up the house and the garden, just as he gave new life to the old furniture that clients entrusted to him. Restoration was his passion. With everything, the famous vitamin C – C for contacts – helped. They managed to buy their place on the waiting list for a Wartburg car from someone they knew. They attached a trailer to the back and drove to Pasewalk to buy what they needed, which was in such short supply: wooden beams for the workshop.

In 1980, as a VEB Perfekt employee, Jutta Janusch was allocated an apartment in Marzahn. Her husband and daughter objected at first, not wanting to leave their old neighbourhood – too sterile, those new buildings, and too far out. But Frau Janusch prevailed – more space, more comfort. Peter Janusch often spent the night at their garden plot over the next few years, as it was only five minutes from his workshop. Maybe the autonomy they both maintained was the recipe for their marriage's success. Every spring, they'd spend a few days on the Baltic coast, usually in Ahrenshoop.

After reunification, VEB Perfekt was liquidated. Frau Janusch was out of a job. She started working for a small leather company in the west of the city. Things also got harder for Herr Janusch. The order book still looked good, but things went downhill on the payment front: 'The easterners paid. But the westerners didn't. That's the way they were – who has the biggest debts? We never imagined it would be like that! And then of course the easterners followed suit.' Herr Janusch still had to bear the operating costs: materials, rent and, above all, his workers' wages. He was at the bottom of his own list, and more and more often he would be left empty-handed. In 1996 Herr Janusch laid off his workers and closed down his business. The furniture workshop was history. He didn't sign on – his pride wouldn't allow it: 'It was a constant bone of contention. Men! They just can't admit it when things go wrong.' Frau Janusch prevailed once more. She sorted out the forms and dragged her husband to the benefits office. From time to time, he'd do some carpentry work for larger companies; he worked in Jamaica for three months. He spent a lot of time on the garden plot, busied himself around the house, built an aviary where he kept pheasants and cockatiels. Frau Janusch told me animals and plants took up more and more of her husband's life.

Illness crept up on him; Herr Janusch took his time going to the doctor. He was diagnosed with chronic pulmonary disease in 2003, at sixty, and Frau Janusch stopped work to look after her husband. Even the slightest physical effort exhausted him. He became thinner and lost his strength. The photo she brought me showed a man on a mobility scooter in front of a guest house on the Baltic coast, in Ahrenshoop: 'He could still go out then.' It was their last minibreak together.

From 2010 onwards, he could no longer leave the apartment. The van would come every Tuesday to refill the two oxygen cylinders, one thirty litres, one forty-five. Frau Janusch grew used to the machines beeping, learned to tell a real alarm from a false alarm. She'd ring the on-call doctor umpteen times a night. She shopped, she cooked. Her husband could only eat things 'that would slip down': mashed potato, rice pudding, soups, apple purée. He didn't want visitors any more, as talking was too hard for him. To stop him getting bored, Frau Janusch bought a computer with her nephew's help, a Mac.

She cleaned, she did the washing, she changed the beds. She ordered medical equipment, arranged doctors' appointments and hospital transport, handed in prescriptions, washed her husband in the shower, cut his hair and his toenails. There were days when Frau Janusch would take the bus for a quick couple of hours on the garden plot to keep on top of things, take care of the bare minimum, and then whizz back home. She once stumbled getting off the bus, broke her left wrist and had to have a plaster cast, and later a splint. Every now and then she too was ill. Her blood pressure went haywire. Her eyes itched with chronic conjunctivitis and the drops she had for ocular hypertension burned. Frau Janusch wore sunglasses to protect her eyes. She didn't make a fuss about her health; she had her husband to look after. She filled out the DNR form and got him to sign it. She sold the car that hadn't been used for years. She went to the woodland cemetery in Bernau, took a guided tour and chose her husband's last resting place.

Peter Janusch died on 20 April 2018, while on morphine at the UKB hospital in Marzahn. He was seventy-five years old. On 6 June he was laid to rest, his urn joining the roots of a copper beech tree: 'Now he's lying under the tree – enough oxygen for him there.'

What Peter and Jutta Janusch had built up together, Jutta Janusch now dismantled on her own. She had the bed, the machines and the oxygen cylinders picked up. She took her husband's clothes to church groups or to the clothes bank. She disposed of medications, hot-water bottles, sheets, shoes; rummaged, sifted and burrowed; tidied, hauled and sorted. She dealt with her husband's books, over 2,000 of them. What she couldn't find a home for, she took to be recycled, bit by bit. It made her sad, especially when it came to his expensive art books. When she'd finished in the apartment, it was time for the garden plot. She unlocked the sheds behind the aviary, where the pheasants and cockatiels had once roosted: 'When

I looked in there, you could have knocked me down with a feather.' Frau Janusch found a complete carpentry workshop: workbenches, tool compartments, petrol chainsaws, wood in all shapes and sizes. On the shelves were tin cans full of nails and screws, hundreds of brand-new dust masks, forty twenty-litre tins of varnish, twenty more tins of mysterious liquid, ten buckets of glue, nineteen bottles of wine, both red and white: 'Those were presents for his clients.' Frau Janusch ordered a skip from the city's waste services for the worst of it. She rang round various hazardous material collection centres. Gave away the tools and the mobility scooter, emptied the wine bottles and became a regular at the recycling centre in Romain-Rolland-Strasse. She would go there with a fully laden wheelbarrow and come back to the garden plot with it empty. Frau Janusch carried her husband's life away, load by load, day by day.

It is now March. Frau Janusch sits on the pink throne as I trim her toenails. Herr Janusch has been dead almost a year. She's never cancelled a chiropody appointment, neither before nor after his death. She still hasn't finished the clearing out: 'I'm getting a little battery chainsaw so I can get rid of the wood.' She doesn't colour her hair any more. It's snow white, cut short, with a pink glow here and there at the ends. Frau Janusch still looks good for her seventy-six years, in spite of the fine lines on her cheeks.

We talk about bras and laugh about how difficult it is to get one that fits. Frau Janusch wants to pick up 'a few bits and pieces' at the shopping centre afterwards. As I massage her feet, she closes her reddened eyes and goes quiet. Suddenly she jerks upright, opens her eyes wide and shouts, 'Green tody! Green tody!' I look up at her, startled. 'What?' I ask. 'Of course, green tody, for God's sake!' she shouts again delightedly. 'It's a Jamaican bird! The password for my husband's Mac! I've been racking my brains for months!' I double up with laughter, Frau Janusch doubles up with laughter, and we laugh and laugh and laugh, as happy as can be, as if the password her head has finally released after eleven months isn't just for a computer, but for something else entirely.

PEGGY AND MIRKO ENGELMANN

I have Struppi to thank for introducing me to Peggy Engelmann. Struppi has a shaggy coat that needs a trim every so often. The lovely woman who runs the dog groomer's around the corner from our salon does it. Struppi is a specimen of the Russian Bolonka Zwetna breed. The name means 'colourful lapdog' and these dogs would fit in almost any handbag. If you were feeling mean-spirited, you might call them ankle-biters.

One day Peggy Engelmann took Struppi for his appointment and came to have her feet done while he was there. We got on straight away. Peggy Engelmann is a warm woman who loves to chat, calls a spade a spade and likes to have the last word. With her wonderful vibrant red shock of hair, she sometimes reminds me of Pippi Longstocking, and sometimes of Mary, Queen of Scots. Peggy Engelmann is forty-two years old and on the way to becoming matronly.

As far as her feet are concerned, there are two problems. First, they are always impeccably looked after, there's no hard skin or cuticles to remove, and her nails are cut and filed flawlessly straight. Second, Peggy's skin has an allergic reaction to pretty much everything, so I can't use bubble bath, foot scrub, our usual creams or even nail oil. In other words, I have nothing to do.

As Peggy Engelmann sat on the throne, she was on her phone sorting out the delivery of her new shoe cupboard, the garden plot owners' association meeting and a breakfast appointment with her grown-up children, who no longer live at home. We chatted and we cackled, and I massaged her feet with a special allergy-friendly cream she had at the ready in her handbag. She arranged two appointments for next time: one for herself and one for her husband, Mirko, in turn, coordinated with Struppi's appointment.

Eight weeks later, Peggy Engelmann took Struppi to the dog groomer's as scheduled, and came to see me at half past four, explaining with a laugh that I mustn't be surprised if she stays in the chiropody room with Mirko; he'd never dare come in on his own.

While Struppi was happy to stay with the lovely woman at the groomer's all on his own, Peggy's forty-five-year-old husband clearly lacked the courage. I had always suspected that Peggy wasn't having her feet done for her own sake, and this was confirmed when Mirko appeared. He arrived at half past five, straight from work, barely said hello to me, gave Peggy a kiss and went off to change into the clean trousers she'd brought from home. He said next to nothing and looked anxiously around at his new surroundings. In preparation for his appointment, he'd cut his nails – typical rookie mistake – but he'd only done eight. Both his big toes were completely naked apart from two tiny scales at his nail roots. I asked Mirko what had happened to his big toes. They had been badly inflamed, explained Peggy, sitting on the chair in the window, and the doctor had made short work of it. I imagined Peggy taking Mirko to the doctor's and sitting beside him the whole time. I held open my gloved hands, exfoliant scrub in each, and when Mirko hesitantly placed his right foot in them, he leaped up from the chair with a yelp. I fell off my stool in shock. 'Of course, I forgot,' squeaked Peggy gleefully, 'he's really ticklish!'

For the rest of the session, the sheepish Mirko silently struggled to keep his composure on the throne. He was half in fits of giggles, half bent over in convulsions. Peggy and I were in stitches.

'How did you two meet?' I asked eight weeks later, as Peggy was sitting on the chair in the window again and Mirko was writhing on the throne. 'My dad set us up,' Peggy said. He was employed as a caretaker at the restaurant where Mirko was working as a chef.

When Peggy paid that evening and arranged the next three-way appointment, we heard a cry of horror in the reception area. We rushed over to find Mirko rooted to the spot in front of the little table with the newspapers. He was staring wide-eyed at Peggy. Tightly clamped between his teeth was a chocolate he'd taken from the glass bowl. Peggy walked over to Mirko as if she was about to kiss him, then sucked the chocolate out of his mouth with her lips and ate it. It was a liqueur chocolate.

When his best friend drank himself to death in 2011, alarm bells began to ring for Mirko. He'd already lost his driving licence, along with his job and the nails on his big toes. Mirko checked into a detox clinic. He was supposed to go for a three-month course of treatment afterwards, but he turned it down, went home and said to Peggy, 'I've got you to help me.' Peggy said, 'This is no time for a rest.' She scoured the job adverts and applied in Mirko's name. After years of unemployment Mirko found work again. He modernizes late-nineteenth-century apartments in Charlottenburg for a property management company: he puts in new windows, rips out walls, installs new bathrooms.

In 2015 Peggy and Mirko set about the task of getting back his driving licence. Mirko had to submit a hair sample every twelve weeks. The hairs always had to be at least six centimetres long. Peggy cut them for him with the help of a ruler. Mirko went to sessions with psychologists and counsellors, and to get his reflexes tested – a dull and costly process, overseen and paid for by Peggy. In early 2017 Mirko was approved for the MPU, the medical and psychological examination, otherwise known as the Idiot Test. He went along. He passed. Unfortunately, they couldn't toast his success. Instead, Peggy and Mirko bought a second car, a little runabout. Mirko wasn't just on the path to recovery, he was now firmly on the open road.

Every day Mirko gets up at the same ungodly hour as Peggy and walks her to her car. He takes Struppi too, so that he can have his first walk of the day (this was Peggy's idea). Sometimes, Mirko rings Peggy up at work five times a day. He's so obedient that he even goes to have his feet done, despite being so ticklish. Mirko's been sober since 2011. He doesn't touch a drop of alcohol. He has replaced the bottle with Peggy, although – or maybe because – Peggy is quite different from a bottle.

She works as a cleaner in a building complex owned by the energy provider Vattenfall. She starts cleaning offices, canteens, control rooms and changing rooms at four in the morning. She's in charge of a cleaning crew of seven people. She organizes, coordinates and delegates, manages, guides and makes decisions. She enjoys it. She has a self-confessed appointment fetish, too much energy, an inability to keep a straight face and a wisdom that impresses me more than any A-grade student's education.

It's a Wednesday in April. Peggy drops Struppi off at the dog groomer's, comes to me at half past four and brings two strawberry tarts that we enjoy together. Peggy always brings something for me, usually a quick energy boost. She looks after me, as she looks after her work colleagues, her children, her dog and her husband. She sits down on the throne and checks the cleaning crew's schedule for the next week on her phone. Then she shows me some photos of her apartment. Mirko is in the process of converting their standard-issue WBS-70 *plattenbau* apartment with its long hallway into a palace, following Peggy's instructions of course. He has already ripped out the wall with the hatch and he's turned their old kitchen and living room into a thirty-metre-square open-plan kitchen-living space, with balcony. As I'm massaging Peggy's feet with the allergy-friendly cream she now keeps in my cupboard, Mirko arrives, gives Peggy a kiss and changes into his clean trousers. He's lost his inhibitions and talks to me nowadays, even when he's writhing and squirming and tensing his feet on the throne, making Peggy and me fall about with laughter as always. Today he's saying that in the old GDR days he fancied a career in the army. Reunification got in the way of that. Even so, Mirko found himself the ideal guiding force: Peggy is better than any sergeant major.

I push aside the magnifying lamp, so that the chiropody room is bathed in a relaxing subdued light. Peggy is sitting on the chair in the window. Mirko's on the throne and, with my firm massage techniques, he finally unwinds. He looks good. Work and abstinence have given him a muscular body without an ounce of fat. Peggy, Mirko and I chat: what happened at work, plans for the next day. As I never have anything to do on her feet, I ask Peggy if she'd like me at least to paint her toenails.

'My sweetie does that,' says Peggy, and smiles at Mirko.

Mirko nods. Mirko grins.

'I've got a steady hand,' he says.

Peggy lets out a giggle from under her shock of red hair, then tells me that Mirko's next project is converting what was the biggest of the children's rooms into their bedroom, with mirrors on the walls and a four-poster bed.

Peggy pays, we arrange a three-way appointment for the end of May and say our goodbyes. I walk the couple to the door, just as the lovely woman from the dog groomer's comes round the corner bringing Struppi, who's wagging his tail with joy at seeing his mistress again, proud of his new haircut.

'This one's all done,' says the lovely woman, pointing to Struppi.

'This one's done too,' says Peggy, and points to Mirko, who pinches her bum. I watch with a hint of envy as Peggy, Struppi and Mirko go off together into the Marzahn evening, attached to each other by imaginary but elaborately intertwined leads.

WRITERS' PUBESCENT DAUGHTERS

A few people of an artistic or intellectual bent, mostly writer girlfriends of mine, take the journey from Prenzlauer Berg, Friedrichshain or Schöneberg to have their feet done in Marzahn. These women don't need my help from a medical perspective, but they do suffer from a lack of attention, or human contact – as do writers' bodies in general (as I know first-hand). It makes little difference whether there's a man in the picture or not. I take on their feet every so often, but I'm not responsible for the rest.

The writers – whether with men in the picture or not – have daughters. These daughters are the real reason the writers visit the salon, because their daughters are hitting puberty. They suffer as their bodies transform, plunging their semi-childlike owners into a state of shame, insecurity and self-doubt. As a consequence, the daughters also find their feet ugly. Their mothers contradict them and assure them that everything is fine with their daughterly feet, but that doesn't make it any better. Not only are the daughters suffering, but they're also clever and they suspect that mothers love everything about their children. Mothers even find the fattest of blackheads adorable. Mothers are not to be believed. The daughters have inherited this cleverness from their mothers, who in turn know that all their concern, their deep sympathy and their great skills of persuasion are unlikely to make their daughters' problems any smaller. A mother's love is a law of nature and doesn't count in their daughters' eyes. And that's why these writers bring their daughters to me. My job is to pass a professional eye over the daughters' supposed problem feet. I send the mothers away and ask them to come back in an hour.

There's Nele sitting on the throne, a fifteen-year-old girl with dark-edged eyes, natural brown curls and flower-like lips for a mouth. Nele is smaller but sharper than her contemporaries. She's skipped a year at school, which makes her seem smaller still than the girls she hangs out with. She thinks she's too fat and round, and she makes the same complaint about her feet. There is nothing wrong with them: they're smooth, they have good circulation and they're flawless, and that's what I tell Nele, who looks out at the world and at me with great solemnity, a solemnity that probably offers her protection. From being underestimated. From being overlooked. From being laughed at. And which helps her to think her way out of uncertainty. I show Nele how well formed her insteps and nails are, and I show her how supple her toes are, by pushing my fingers between them. Would Nele like her nails varnished? Yes, she'll give it a go, although like her mother she doesn't think much of make-up or getting dressed up. But she doesn't want red, she doesn't want clichéd or kitsch nail polish, picking instead an ice blue. And that's what she gets. When she leaves, what I get is Nele's solemn, beautiful face breaking into a confiding smile.

There's Isabell, just turned seventeen, five foot ten and probably not yet fully grown. She moves gracefully like a young mare. She's tied back her strong, healthy hair into a stout ponytail and I ask if I can feel it for a moment, as I like its ample thickness so much. Isabell doesn't just have long hair, she also has long hands with long fingers and long feet with long toes. As if that wasn't enough, her mother sent me a long email to prepare me for the appointment, describing her daughter's foot concerns in detail and taking the blame herself – her feet grew quickly, she always needed new shoes which were not always bought promptly and not always of the best quality. Isabell now only wears clumpy men's shoes, even in summer, to hide her feet. She thinks her toenails are too thick, which isn't true. It could be true at some point in the future if she doesn't free her feet from those men's shoes. I heap praise on her graceful, slender hands, which could belong to a pianist, and I ask Isabell if it's ever occurred to her that every person's hands and feet suit each other perfectly. Isabell is polite and well brought up, but she cannot hide a slight scepticism towards this place she's ended up in, opposite this woman who's supposed to be a writer but now earns her crust here. She must be scared it'll be her mother next.

There's Natalie, twelve years old and caught in that temporary state where her limbs are disproportionate, all puppy fat and growth spurts. Almond eyes. High cheekbones. A little birthmark like a beauty spot over the left corner of her mouth, a mouth that sometimes smirks, giving her a mischievous look when combined with a raised eyebrow. Natalie does a funny imitation of how she thinks women behave and talk when they are among themselves, at the hairdresser's, for instance. She becomes a chatterbox, drawing me into her confidence, discussing her role in school projects, her budgies' personalities and matters of fashion. Her feet are perfectly fine, but Natalie thinks they look pasty. I spread her toes into a fan, show her how strong her Achilles tendon is and, just for fun, point out the line her Lisfranc joints take. In the old days when knights on horseback fell out of their stirrups, this is the area that would break from the impact, and nowadays it's where forefoot amputation starts, because then they don't need to use a bone saw. The child reacts to these grisly details with a blush, her cheeks matching the cherry-red nail varnish I'm applying. We paint another layer of glitter over the top.

They don't want to show it, but their faces give them away: they marvel, alternately at their feet and then at me, these writers' pubescent daughters. They mull over what an odd friend Mum has, what a weird job it is, concerning yourself with other people's appendages. Their eyes wander back and forth between me and the feet in my hands, the feet that become alien in the light from the magnifying lamp but palpably remain their own, and clearly merit being looked at, discussed and touched.

I also quietly marvel at them: at their purity, the smoothness of their skin and the charm that shines through on their faces. Lolitas, on the verge of blooming. Their ignorance of their own beauty only makes them more beautiful.

My favourite is Mizzi, the little sister of one of the writers' pubescent daughters. Mizzi is five, the opposite number to the ninety-six-year-old Frau Noll Senior in my gallery of clients. Mizzi finds it far easier to climb up on the throne than many grown men do. She is an unusual child, as she loves dentists; in this respect I'm at an advantage with my white clothes, my gloves and instruments. She intently follows what I'm doing with a professional interest and when it tickles she gets annoyed, because she needs to laugh and can't pay attention. Sometimes I keep tickling her anyway, because I can't get enough of her exuberant, full-body laughter, her hair shaking like a mop, her milk teeth and her uvula exposed. At the end I brush a bright pink onto her tiny nails and, while it's drying, I ask her to open her mouth, push in a little bar of Kinder chocolate and look on at my completely satisfied customer enthroned on her much-too-big throne. Once, her mother told me, Mizzi had a friend round from preschool and wanted to play chiropodists. The friend didn't know what that meant and Mizzi, clearly baffled, asked, 'What? You've never been to the chiropodist?'

GERLINDE BONKAT

The number of refugees in the Marzahn-Hellersdorf district is high in comparison to other areas of Berlin. There are currently 3,384 living here, 15.15 per cent of all the refugees on record in the city.

I know one of the refugees who lives in Marzahn, one who's been in Germany for quite some time and who, I suspect, isn't included in these statistics for that very reason. First name: Gerlinde. Surname: Bonkat. Date of birth: 25 May 1938. Birthplace: Königsberg (now Kaliningrad).

Not even seven years old and having only just started school, Gerlinde Bonkat fled westward from East Prussia in January 1945 with her mother and her three-year-old brother. Gerlinde's father had been conscripted into the Wehrmacht in 1943. On the journey Gerlinde wore Igelit plastic shoes, which would expand with the heat in summer and break with the cold in winter. Her mother had packed the bare essentials in two suitcases and she'd sewn rucksacks for her children. Gerlinde, her mother and her brother boarded a ship called the *Lappland* in Pillau (now Baltiysk). On board, people crowded onto bunk beds. Gerlinde, inquisitively wandering around on deck, was shouted at by sailors and sent back to her mother. The three of them perched on a top bunk. An old lady lay on the bunk below. Gerlinde watched her and at one point whispered to her mother, 'I think the lady's dead.' Her mother called one of the crew. The old lady was taken from the bed and put in a sack. The sack containing the old lady was added to the other sacks containing other corpses.

Later on, the sailors distributed life jackets; the ship was taking on water. It reached the port of Swinemünde (now Świnoujście), where it was evacuated. Crowds of people pushed their way on to land, in the midst of them Gerlinde, her mother, her brother and two suitcases. Gerlinde saw the corpses in sacks being hauled ashore. She didn't see what happened to them next. But she was pleased at any rate – she'd spent the whole time imagining the dead might simply be thrown overboard into the Baltic.

Gerlinde Bonkat is now eighty years old. She lives on the tenth floor of an eleven-storey Marzahn block near our salon. Frau Bonkat and I have a special arrangement: she comes to see me for half an hour once a fortnight. She's happy to take any appointment I can offer her. She always arrives on time. Whether it's the height of summer or the depths of winter, she stands outside the door. When I open it she smiles and holds out her hand, and I press it, just very gently. Then I carefully lift the strap of her shoulder bag from her left shoulder and over her head, help her out of her coat and take her little plastic bag, its print long since worn off though the bag still fulfils its purpose. I unpack the bag in the chiropody room: a towel, a tube of Voltarol, clean pop socks. Frau Bonkat takes a seat in the chiropody chair; she's always happy to be able to sit down. She takes off her shoes – comfortable flat beige shoes without complicated fastenings – and puts her feet in the water.

In Swinemünde, where the leaky *Lappland* had anchored, the three of them were crammed into a schoolhouse with hundreds of other people. They sat on the cellar steps, day and night, and were grateful to be given even a weak coffee. They had nothing to eat. Her mother took a bar of chocolate out of her bag and said Gerlinde and her brother could share half of it. Gerlinde said, 'But it's not Dieter's birthday yet!' 'It doesn't matter,' said her mother.

They were bundled onto a goods train that was packed with people and windowless like cattle transport. On the way, one of the two suitcases went missing and with it their family album, with photos of her father. When they got off the goods train, they were in Denmark. It was the first time Gerlinde saw her mother cry.

The refugee camp was enormous. There were ten barracks for every letter of the alphabet. 'Don't forget the barrack number,' said her mother. Sometimes she went to help in the camp kitchen and then she might come back with a cabbage stalk for the children. For her brother's birthday, her mother made a horse out of some fabric from an old military coat. For its mane, she cut off a tuft of her own hair. Gerlinde and her brother played in the camp, fenced in with barbed wire. No refugees were allowed to leave. Gerlinde pestered her mother, because she wanted to go back to school. Her mother wrote to an uncle in Germany appealing for help.

As Frau Bonkat sits on the chair, she exudes the unperfumed, simple old-fashioned soapy cleanliness I loved about my grandma. I take the same care washing her feet as I did pressing her hand. Frau Bonkat's asymmetric feet look like my disposable gloves when I pull them off and drop them carelessly in the bin. Her toes point in all directions, overlap each other, some long, some reduced to half their size. Feet that have been crippled. On her left foot, a pronounced bunion like an overripe tuber glows red. Her big toe tilts at a right angle, over the smaller sidekick next to it. The bunion on her right foot was operated on. Ever since, her right second toe has been missing a phalanx bone and her basal toe joint has been pressing on her dropped transverse arch. Frau Bonkat practically walks on bone. Under the pressure of this bone, she has a hard, circular corn so clearly defined that I call it her trolley token. Every step is painful for Frau Bonkat, but this doesn't stop her walking.

In the summer of 1947, two and a half years after leaving East Prussia with two suitcases, Gerlinde, her mother and her brother arrived at the uncle's in Altentreptow, nine miles from Neubrandenburg. There were already four people living in the uncle's room and now there would be seven. But at least Gerlinde could go to school. She would be ten years old on her next birthday and should have been in the fourth year. It was agreed she would go into the year below. Her mother impressed on her, 'We are refugees. Refugees have to make double, triple the effort.' Gerlinde made the effort and caught up in a few weeks. During breaks, when the other children were playing in the playground, she'd practise cross-multiplication with the maths teacher. Once, she argued with her German teacher over how to write a 't'. She had learned it differently in Königsberg. The teacher held out; Gerlinde complied.

Her mother worked on a farm, then in a clothing factory as a cleaner. Gerlinde fended for herself, looked after her little brother and helped around the house. Sundays were the only days off. Sundays were holy. The three of them spent Sundays together. They would go to church, read stories to each other, sing songs. Her mother taught Gerlinde lace knitting. They'd sit together, and Gerlinde would talk about her friends, her teachers and school. In the evenings they'd pray.

There was no trace of her father, even after the GDR came into existence. They passed around a passport photo of him, to no avail. They had no evidence of his death and even less faith that he might have survived.

When Gerlinde was fourteen, her mother said, 'You needn't imagine you'll carry on with your education.' Gerlinde asked why. She would have liked to do her exams when she turned sixteen or even go on to take the next ones at eighteen. She was getting good marks. Her mother simply said, 'We are Christians.'

In 1953, having been at school for six years and completed the fifth form, Gerlinde left school and home. She was fifteen years old. She began a three-year secretarial training course at the Evangelical Konsistorium in Greifswald.

In 1955 Gerlinde wrote a letter to Wilhelm Pieck, the GDR's first president: it had been ten years since they had left East Prussia, her mother worked hard, her brother went to school, the two of them and a married couple still shared a connecting room in Altentreptow, didn't he think it was time they had an apartment? Of course, there was no reply from Wilhelm Pieck. But two years later, in 1957, her mother was allocated an apartment: nothing more than a single room with a kitchen, cold and draughty, but nonetheless a place of her own. She was still working in the clothing factory in Altentreptow; she had progressed from cleaner to bookkeeper. Gerlinde assumed her letter had helped.

Once I've dried her feet, I send Frau Bonkat and the chair up in the air and tilt it slightly backwards. I position the magnifying lamp over her right foot, spray callus softener on her trolley token, stretch it with my left hand and remove layers of hard skin from the outside in, with the scalpel parallel to her skin. Every so often I pause, look up at Frau Bonkat and ask if it hurts. Frau Bonkat shakes her head and carries on talking. She formulates crystal-clear, quotable sentences and speaks an accentless German, with a faintly Nordic hint to its melody. It's only sometimes, when she's very deeply absorbed in her East Prussian past, that she suddenly rolls an 'r' like an old sea dog. When she's thinking, she raises her head, her ears exposed by her short hair. She has a lively face with fine features. Her alert eyes look up out of deep hollows into the distance. I could listen to Frau Bonkat for hours on end when she talks about old times. About that journey, about her mother, about the refugee camp, about the children's home.

Gerlinde finished her secretarial training, but she wanted to become a nurse. Nursing was a family tradition. She spotted a small advert in a church magazine and applied to the Diaconal Sisterhood in Berlin. When she arrived there, she wasn't given any training but was sent straight to a church-run children's home in the middle of a forest near Strausberg. She landed on her feet and embarked there and then on her second career. At first she was responsible for the 'tots', those less than a year old, and later for the bigger ones, who were up to five years old. The children in the home came from illegitimate relationships. Some of the mothers secretly visited their children. There were no fathers. The woman in charge told Gerlinde not to grow too fond of the children.

One morning in October, Gerlinde was on the early shift, which started at four. It was an unusually cold autumn, minus twenty degrees at night; it had been snowing. Gerlinde switched on the ground-floor lights and pushed open the door of the children's home, intending to clear the snow in front of it. She hit an object with the tip of her shoe and stepped over it. She bent down, felt something, freed it from the snow and unwrapped it. A newborn baby, freezing, red and blue. Gerlinde ran into the house with the child in her arms, poured out some water from the bathwater heater, still warm from the night before, and shouted for the caretaker. She let the baby cry, so that life would return to it. It was a boy.

The doctor was called, examined the baby and declared the day he was found to be his birthday. The police came and Gerlinde had to describe what had happened. 'I found him under the snow,' she said. The social welfare office needed a name so that a case file could be opened. All the staff looked to Gerlinde, who said, 'Peter.' And his surname? '*Heute ist Freitag*,' someone else said: 'today is Friday.' From then on, the boy's name was Peter Freitag. The staff brought him up until he was six. Then the same thing happened to Peter Freitag that happened to all the children in the home. When the time came for them to start school, they were taken away and allocated to state children's homes. The staff were never told where.

Gerlinde was barely twenty and an unskilled childcare assistant when she found Peter Freitag. Soon after that she went on to Rostock for training. She lived in the college, learned education theory and psychology, and studied the Old and New Testaments.

After her exam Gerlinde went to a church home in Rostock, once again looking after children thrown on the scrapheap. She was responsible for fifteen boys between the ages of three and eighteen with learning disabilities. Sometimes she'd play football with them. The soles came away from her black lace-up shoes and Gerlinde went to the cobbler's. The cobbler showed her how to kick a ball and keep her shoes in one piece, but Gerlinde couldn't get the hang of it. Over and over she would go back to the cobbler's with broken shoes for him to glue back together.

From 1960 to 1962, Gerlinde trained for her third career, the one she'd always wanted. She became a nurse in the Evangelical Hospital of Queen Elisabeth Herzberge in Berlin. She wore a nurse's hat, a grey dress and a grey apron, and on her feet the same black lace-ups that had been glued so often by the Rostock cobbler. When a patient died, she would write their name, date of birth and date of death on a label and tie it around their big toe. At first, she lived in the hospital, as there were rooms for the nurses, then she found a room to rent in Leninallee, and later on again she moved into a one-room apartment in an old building in Matternstrasse in Friedrichshain, at the rear of the building, with a coal stove and the loo on the landing. Gerlinde didn't earn much. With what she had left in her pay packet, she'd buy toothpaste one month, shoe polish the next. She put most of it by for concert tickets. She loved classical music. She didn't think of herself as poor. Money has never played a big part in Gerlinde's life.

When I've removed the trolley token from her right forefoot, I move on to the two problem areas on her left foot – an ingrown toenail and a pressure point on a hammer toe. Sometimes we sing together, Frau Bonkat and I, to take her mind off the pain – the old German folk song '*Winter adé, Scheiden tut weh*'. She once brought a piece of paper on which she'd written out a story word for word with a ballpoint pen, copied from a book. While I was massaging Voltarol into her feet, she read the story aloud to me. It was about a little boy who dreamed of a garden. Another time she gave me a calendar with papercut pictures. I've given her a book about wolves and an ointment to keep the pressure point on her hammer toe soft.

In 1964 Gerlinde swapped her grey nurse's uniform for a white coat. She moved to a state hospital in Friedrichshain and started working with the doctor in charge. She filled out one of her usual toe labels and tied it on. By doing that, she had overstepped her authority. Only doctors were allowed to certify deaths in this hospital. While the doctor in charge was on the phone furiously shouting at her, just like the sailors on board the *Lappland* had done, a smiling Gerlinde held out the receiver so everyone in the nurses' room could hear. She complied with conventions, as she'd done with the 't', although she never lost her ability to establish that a person had died.

Gerlinde worked in the Friedrichshain hospital's gynaecology department for five years, before she was taken on by a rheumatologist in Buch, where the Charité Hospital ran a rheumatology clinic. From there, she moved on to a polyclinic in Mitte, to assist a general practitioner. For a long time, she was a nurse in a retirement home. Then she went back to children once more. Working for the school welfare service, she would lug big bags of instruments and vaccines on buses and trains all over Berlin to give classes their smallpox boosters.

After twenty years of nursing, Gerlinde's feet simply couldn't take any more. At the age of forty-three, she left the profession and went back to being a secretary. Every day she went to Schönhauser Allee, where she soon became the director's secretary at the Inner Mission, a Christian initiative.

Gerlinde came to Marzahn in 1981. She was among the first people to be allocated one of the sought-after apartments in the *plattenbau* estate in the east of East Berlin, which at that time was an enormous treeless building site. Gerlinde was given the one-room apartment on the tenth floor where she still lives today: thirty-six square metres, with balcony. She joined the evangelical church in Marzahn and went to services and concerts at the village church in Alt-Marzahn.

She's always gone to church, either in Altentreptow, where she often visited her mother, or in Berlin, joining whichever one was near where she lived. She's always taken the concept of 'congregation' literally: 'You can't have Jesus without the church. Alone you are not a Christian.' She's made friends, helped people and received help. She's met up with old and new friends and acquaintances, for walks, for concerts, for a coffee. Until his death, she even kept in contact with the maths teacher with whom she had practised cross-multiplication during breaks, and with the German teacher she'd argued with over the 't'. Gerlinde has always lived alone; she has never been lonely.

I once asked Frau Bonkat if the GDR, where she spent most of her working life, had become a home for her. 'No,' she replied. 'Königsberg is my home.' That was why so many moves and job changes hadn't bothered her. She always liked working, always looked for new challenges, always carried on learning. 'It didn't really matter where. I am a refugee. Right now, I'm here.'

When the Wall came down, Gerlinde was fifty-one years old. She remembered what her mother used to say in the GDR's early years, when socialism was being established at full speed: 'They can't recreate mankind.'

Gerlinde changed jobs again, this time involuntarily. The Inner Mission, where she'd become the director's secretary, was combined with the West Berlin branch and became a deaconry again. From 1993 onwards, Gerlinde travelled from Marzahn to Steglitz every day, a longer commute. The bouquet of flowers that greeted every new colleague back in the old East seemed not to exist here. Instead, Gerlinde had to listen to the words, 'We know you don't have any proper training, but we might get used to you.' No one read her CV. Not for the first time in her life, Gerlinde felt foreign, but she was not intimidated. She found ways and means to show her colleagues how hard she could work. For the first time, it gave her no pleasure. The ignorance and the arrogance of her colleagues from the West made her hackles rise.

One day, though, after five years, her boss in Steglitz glanced at Gerlinde's CV. 'But you're overqualified!' he shouted. 'You know,' Gerlinde said with quiet satisfaction, 'it doesn't hurt.'

With that, Gerlinde left the world of work. In 1998, at the age of sixty, she retired. There was an exhaustion that went way beyond her feet. Her pension was minimal, but she was used to thrift.

Gerlinde the nurse became a patient herself at that time, when she had the bunion on her right foot operated on. At her check-up with the doctor after a few weeks, he looked at her foot and asked, 'Did I do that?' The operation was a complete failure: her foot hurt more than ever before.

When I carefully rub Frau Bonkat's feet with Voltarol, she appreciates the easing of her pain, although it never completely disappears. She says the hideous shoes she wore as a child are only half the root of her ailments. The other half was inherited. All the women in her family have loose joints, stretched ligaments or weak tendons. One cousin developed a bunion by the time she was eleven. 'Our wretched bones are good for nothing,' she told me. I have a vision of an entire squad of Bonkat nurses, all with white nurse's hats and grey aprons, black sandals peeking out from under the grey fabric of their dresses, revealing their bare feet with bunions like overripe tubers, glowing red.

I ask Frau Bonkat why she's never had a family of her own. There wasn't a lack of advances from men. In her youth, Frau Bonkat says, it was quite different from now. A married woman had to bring up the children and run the house, serve her husband and take a subordinate role. As she was completely wrapped up in her work, it was never something she felt like doing. 'I've never liked being told what to do.' Frau Bonkat was already emancipated at a time when the word was still relatively unknown.

*

After reunification, she made one last attempt to get to the bottom of her father's fate, writing to the German Red Cross Tracing Service in Munich, the office responsible for searching for people who went missing in the Second World War. They wrote back: there was no information available.

In 2001, when she walked into the little Altentreptow apartment, there was a smell of death. Gerlinde was familiar with the smell. She climbed into bed with her mother. They talked, they sang, they prayed. 'Are you still there?' her mother asked. 'Yes,' said Gerlinde. 'Will you hold me?' her mother asked. 'Yes,' said Gerlinde. 'That's lovely,' her mother said. Then she died in Gerlinde's arms. Gerlinde folded her mother's arms, tied her chin up to close her mouth, then rang her brother and the other relatives.

Gerlinde tore her right bicep in 2004, trying to open a bottle. In 2007 she tore her left bicep too, with no apparent cause. Ever since, the bone in her upper arm has been forming a lump under her skin. A doctor diagnosed a diaphragmatic hernia, saying, 'Frau Bonkat, your wrinkles aren't just on the outside.'

Two years ago, Frau Bonkat bent down, just as she'd done all those years ago outside the children's home at four in the morning, to pick up a piece of fluff from the carpet; this broke her coccyx. She still managed to get to the salon, taking one step at a time on crutches, and when I asked her if I should take her crutches, she corrected me, her eyes flashing for a moment, 'We're not meant to call them crutches. They're walking aids!'

I admire the fact that she's never seen herself as a victim – a quality that makes her utterly anachronistic. I like it when she starts mouthing off. I like her firm, clear opinions. You can sense something tangible about Frau Bonkat, something that goes beyond the fragile woman with the weak bones. It's faith, that great constant in her life: her faith. Since I've known Frau Bonkat, I've been listening out for the Marzahn church bells.

She still goes to church every Sunday. It used to take her ten minutes to walk to Alt-Marzahn, but now it's half an hour. Only when it's rainy or stormy does she give it a miss, as she can't hold up an umbrella.

Frau Bonkat hasn't been able to lift her arms very high since she tore her biceps. She reminds me of a marionette with its strings cut, or a broken-winged angel. If she wants to comb her hair, she bends her upper body down until her hands can reach her head, while her upper arms simply hang in mid-air. On Fridays a woman she knows brings her shopping and helps her take a shower. Another friend helps her change the sheets, a job she says would take her four hours if she had to do it herself. A young woman comes and cleans; a young man takes her washing away and brings it back. Twice a week Frau Bonkat goes to a physiotherapist, who massages her right arm. She comes to see me once a fortnight. Our half-hour usually lasts longer.

I stretch her fresh pop socks over her feet and help her into her comfortable flat beige shoes without complicated fastenings. They look smart, although, as Frau Bonkat puts it, they are 'a few Thursdays old'. I pack her things into the little plastic bag with the worn-off print. I help her into her coat and carefully lift the strap of her shoulder bag over her head and onto her left shoulder. I say goodbye with a gentle press of the hand and open the door for her. She smiles and walks off slowly, slightly bent forward, her hands folded behind her.

In the spring, she loves the yellow of the dandelions on the grass in front of our salon; in the autumn, the chestnuts galore that lie under the tree. Once, a cute little boy noticed Frau Bonkat standing by the chestnuts and asked if she'd collected some. She said she hadn't. The little boy gathered two handfuls of chestnuts and put them in Frau Bonkat's shoulder bag for her. Delighted, she took the chestnuts home and put them in a wooden bowl.

At night, if Frau Bonkat wakes up, she goes onto the balcony of her one-room apartment on the tenth floor. At four in the morning, with the Marzahn tower blocks quiet and dark at her feet, she lifts up her head and looks at the last star visible before dawn, the morning star. She never heard anything more about Peter Freitag. She assumes he must be out there somewhere in the world. He'd be in his sixties now.

There's a lost nun in Frau Bonkat – a nun without a convent, an emancipated nun in her natural habitat. A *plattenbau* nun.

I want to pay tribute to Gerlinde Bonkat's lifetime achievement, because if I don't no one else will. She has seized every opportunity to make up for her difficult start in life, defending her independence to this day. She is a refugee who doesn't appear in current statistics and who's owned very few pairs of shoes over her lifetime. First from poverty, then from frugality and now because a broken-in pair of shoes is worth its weight in gold.

In November 1944 a letter circuitously reached her mother in Königsberg. Gerlinde's father wrote that he'd been transferred from Norway and was stationed in a village in East Prussia. Her mother packed some food into a rucksack, took his boots, which were far too big for her, stuffed them with newspaper and put them on. She set off, through the cold, through the mud. When she arrived in the village, Gerlinde's father wasn't there. She asked around. No one knew what had become of him. Her mother shared out the food meant for him with the other soldiers and then made her way back home through the cold and the mud with an empty rucksack. Arriving home, she told Gerlinde and her brother she'd looked for their father but hadn't found him. Then she took his boots off.

HERR AND FRAU HUTH

Marzahn Park Cemetery, eight in the morning. The sun blinks through the thick canopy of leaves. The grass is still damp from the night and the air's so fresh you could almost bite into it. I wander along the rows of graves, gaze at the plants, read the inscriptions. Many Russians are buried here, as well as born-and-bred Berliners; you can tell by their names. Herr Paulke, my former client, also rests here. A jay is screeching, songbirds are rejoicing, two squirrels are chasing each other. A magnolia is shedding its petals like confetti. It's lovely to start the day in a deserted cemetery. I move on and cross the old S-Bahn bridge, because I have to get to work. It takes me ten minutes to walk through the estate and reach the tower block and the beauty salon.

Frau Huth is an energetic, rotund person, a Berliner through and through. She's lived in Marzahn with her husband for thirty years, not far from the salon. Her feet are just as small and solid as she is, and she is extremely sensitive where her nerves end, under the front edges of her nails. She keeps her own nail varnish in my cupboard, a coral red that I use on her toenails when it's warm enough for her to wear her white slip-on sandals. Frau Huth digs out a magnifying glass from her large handbag to inspect the results. She has been through all kinds of eye operations: 'Still can't see, though. But they're not getting me under the knife again, they've earned enough from me already.'

I like Frau Huth's unsentimental manner. She is on the ball, she talks quickly, she even laughs quickly, with an infectious, bleating sound, and her eyes flick back and forth constantly like hockey pucks, as if they don't want to miss the slightest thing. Frau Huth would never have the time to wander through the cemetery for a while in the mornings, like I do. She is eighty-three years old and always on the go, twenty-four hours a day.

When I first met her, I always wished she'd take a break, at least for the hour she spent in the chiropody chair, just for that one hour at least. I'd massage her feet and remind her to relax her muscles, but Frau Huth always seemed in a rush. She'd worry that her husband would leave the apartment to go and look for his wife, and get lost, and then it would be her having to look for him. She'd run out of the salon before the coral-red varnish on her toenails was completely dry. She'd find her husband in places he had known for thirty years: in front of the chemist's, by the fruit and veg stall at the weekly market, or outside the bank, where he once stood handing out money to passers-by. She'd take him by the hand and walk him home.

After that, she drew a clock on a sheet of paper for her husband. She drew the big hand pointing to the nine, put the sheet on the table in the living room and drummed it into her husband that he had to wait until the big hand on the wall clock pointed to the nine as well. Then he could go and pick her up from the chiropodist's. It didn't work. Herr Huth stood, lost, 100 metres further on, outside the hairdresser's where Frau Huth had been getting her hair done for the last thirty years.

I suggested bringing her husband along with her. So while she was having her pedicure, he sat in the wicker chair in the reception area and read a newspaper. Or, more strictly speaking, he held the newspaper up so that it looked like he was reading it. 'Makes no difference what's in it,' said Frau Huth, and we giggled. She said he always sat like that at home too, on the sofa, which was fine by her, because she could get the housework done quickly. 'He always wants to help with the housework,' she moaned, rolling her lively eyes. She used to give him the hoovering to do, but not any more; it was beyond him now. So Frau Huth kitted him out with some bathroom cleaner and a sponge. Ever since, he's been polishing the sink up to six times a day. 'You wouldn't believe how shiny it is!' she said, laughing her infectious laugh.

Frau Huth called out to her husband from the chiropody room: 'Gerhard!' And then, more insistently, 'Gerhard!' Herr Huth, who is very hard of hearing, stayed where he was. I went to fetch him. He looked hesitantly around the door. He saw his wife's bare feet sitting in a bowl full of water and bubbles. He said, 'I thought you were getting your hair done!' There's no room in Herr Huth's dementia-ridden brain for the chiropody treatment Frau Huth's been having for the last three years. Every time he stands outside our door, hand in hand with his wife, it's the first time.

It's always half past twelve, according to Herr Huth's watch. Once, he tapped on its glass as if he'd be able to bring the hands back to life, shook his wrist and held the watch up to his all but deaf ear. He shrugged. 'Nothing to be done,' he said, and it made me think of *Waiting for Godot*, when Estragon shakes out his boot and Vladimir knocks on his bowler hat.

The next time, I offered Herr Huth a seat in the chiropody room, by the window. Frau Huth took a joke book from the shelf and handed it to her husband, who obediently opened it. As Frau Huth was dipping her feet into the footbath, Herr Huth looked up from the book in astonishment and said, 'I thought you were getting your hair done!' Frau Huth and I giggled. Herr Huth lowered his head and looked blankly at the book, never turning a page, and never laughing. 'I don't find the jokes in that book funny either,' I said. Frau Huth shook her head and said that lately he kept falling asleep all the time, no matter where he was.

Frau Huth always worked full-time, first in an office, then in a delicatessen in Leipziger Strasse. She had three children, and when her sister died at an early age, she took on her two children as well and brought them up with her own. Frau Huth has never trusted any system, neither socialism nor capitalism; she was always a little afraid for her children and, like a lioness, made sure that her family returned safely to the kitchen table every night. When Frau Huth retired, her husband became ill with prostate cancer and a hospital odyssey began: operations, radiotherapy, chemotherapy, medication to combat the side effects and other medical treatments. The cancer spread throughout his entire body and arrangements were made for the next procedure, to cut away half of his upper jaw. Frau Huth decided that enough was enough. No more operations. Since then, Herr Huth has been classed as having exhausted all forms of therapy. Three or four times a week, hand in hand with his wife, he goes to the dentist's in Friedrichshain, where they take care of the affected parts of his mouth. 'I can't do this much longer,' Frau Huth says quietly. Then adds, 'He's always looked after us so well.' Herr Huth is Frau Huth's last child, albeit one who can't be sent to a kindergarten or a club. 'A care home's out of the question,' says Frau Huth, true to her mistrust of all systems, authorities and institutions.

Sometimes, Frau Huth tells me, Herr Huth has clear moments. At night, when he can't sleep, he lies awake next to his wife and asks her what she's still doing there with him, now that he has nothing left to offer her. On nights like that, Herr Huth cries, and I can fully understand it – the clear moments are the worst.

Last week, Herr Huth had the first pedicure of his life. He sat on the chiropody chair and said, as I was washing his feet, 'I've got size eleven feet. I have big shoes to fill.' Frau Huth and I giggled, and then Frau Huth, who was sitting on the chair in the window, turned and looked out. I trimmed Herr Huth's toenails, cleaned his nail folds, smoothed the edges of his nails with the drill and filed his heels. He slept. He looked pale and peaceful. Frau Huth pulled her magnifying glass out of her big handbag, inspecting and touching her freshly painted coral-red toenails. 'Dry,' she said, and slipped on her white sandals. I massaged Herr Huth's feet, which were supple and flexible. He woke up. He looked around, confused, peered at me, peered at his feet, peered back at me. Frau Huth stood up, went over to the chiropody chair and took her husband's hand. Herr Huth recognized Frau Huth. 'I thought I was getting my hair cut,' he said.

In Samuel Beckett's play, the two tramps, Vladimir and Estragon, are waiting for Godot. But Godot never comes. Ever since *Waiting for Godot* was first performed in Paris in 1953, actors, directors, dramatists, theatre scholars and philosophers have been racking their brains over who Godot could be. I don't think Herr Huth would be familiar with the play. But maybe he knows who Godot is.

Marzahn Park Cemetery, eight in the evening, far from the noise of the city. At the end of a hot, dusty day, the birds are singing their evening chorus. The sun is at a low angle, its last rays spreading like wings over names on individual stones. Raked paths. Watered graves. Burning candles. Larches, oaks, pines. I wander through ferns and across the grass in the shade. Coolness, peace and space. A birch. A bench. It's lovely to end the day in a deserted cemetery.

Are they over, those fuzzy years? Those years when you were thrashing about in the middle of a big lake, turning around at a loss, flagging from the tedium of swimming? When fear set in, of sinking halfway, without a sound, without a cause? Is your bleak midlife crisis over?

I think so.

You're almost fifty and you've realized that the time for you to do the things you want to do is now, not later. It might be an old self-help-book platitude, but it's true all the same. You're almost fifty and you're even more invisible than you were: ideal conditions for doing those things, be they terrible, wonderful or peculiar. Against the chiropody room's white walls, you're so invisible in your white clothes that you can mirror your colourful clients, unnoticed, as they're sitting on the pink throne. You spend all your time laughing with them, all your time thinking about them and sometimes you look them in the eye. When you're standing at the M6 tram stop in your dark clothes with your hair down, your clients don't recognize you.

*

When Marzahn was created in the last century, in the 70s, the civil engineering collective built walk-through underground tunnels through which the pipes and cables for district heating, water, electricity and communication run. Six miles of underworld; 340 manholes. No one has to dig up the earth if something needs repairing. In an emergency, Marzahners can always escape through these concrete tunnels.

In my opinion, Marzahn's shopping centre is the finest in all Berlin. The hospital in Marzahn has the best A&E department, which has saved not only some of my clients' lives, but also my partner's, one June night at half past three in the morning. The council offices in Marzahn are paradise compared to the council offices in Friedrichshain-Kreuzberg. The Marzahn waste disposal services have already taken away the New Year's rubbish, while they're still setting off the fireworks in Mitte. In the Biertulpe bar, a small Berliner Pilsner costs just one sixty and a large one two euros. Genz the butcher's in Alt-Marzahn makes the most exquisite cheesy meatballs. The post is still delivered every day in Marzahn. Sadly, though, Marzahn doesn't have enough doctors: they're getting old themselves and going into retirement. The ones who are left don't have the resources to cope with the hordes of ill people.

Since early 2015, I've taken care of approximately 3,800 feet, in other words 19,000 toes. I've held every single one of those toes between my thumb and forefinger in a pincer grip.

I've got myself some new work shoes. After four years, the white Birkenstocks I bought for my training in the

Charlottenburg academy were past it. My new work shoes are still essentially white, but printed all over with 'little pink flowers', as it says in English on the box. Quite bold, by my standards. Flocke and Tiffy love them.

My daughter lives in Heidelberg, where she's studying and in love. Wouldn't be surprised if I'm a grandma soon.

My partner is getting back to his healthy self, as far as possible after all his illnesses. In his old age, he's gone back to the place he was born. We visit each other. We speak on the phone.

I am at home here in Berlin, on my floating island in Marzahn. The love I have inside me has turned to liquid and now runs into the most unlikely places. The bitterness I was carrying around has disappeared, along with the last remainders of youthful arrogance. In their place, I can detect the onset of a mellowing with age, which can sometimes lead to a slight tendency towards kitsch (see 'little pink flowers' above). I don't care. No one can see me.

It's a Wednesday morning at the end of January. From four to six, I sit at my writing desk. Then I hop into the shower, make some sandwiches and pack my rucksack. I leave home at half past seven and buy tram tickets and three pieces of cake on the way – one for Tiffy, one for Flocke and one for me. Children are going to school; builders are drinking coffee. It's just getting light. It's cold. People are scraping the hoar frost from their windscreens. I reach the tram stop. The M6 comes every five minutes at this time of day. There are grey faces inside the tram. I pick a window seat, as always. My journey takes twenty-one minutes. More grey faces get on at Landsberger Allee S-Bahn station, bundled up in hats and hoods. Figures with phones, earphones, prams. Figures ignoring each other completely. I like these brief tram shares. I don't know where the others are going, but I always look forward to my work, even if I'm dog-tired, even if there's tension in the salon. I know that, somehow, I'll always get through it. I've never yet arrived late. I always have the day's schedule in my head. Today I have eight clients: 9 a.m. Hattenhauer; 10 a.m. Bonkat; 11 a.m. Hannelore Müller; 12.30 p.m. Jürgen; 2 p.m. Arndt; 3 p.m. Sabine Schulz; 5 p.m. Kluge; 6 p.m. Ponesky (met by Frau Frenzel, Amy and Leila afterwards).

Frau Bonkat came two weeks ago and was having more trouble walking than usual, her face worn from the pain in her hip. Will she have seen the doctor since then? You can never tell with Frau Bonkat. As a nun in her natural habitat, she'll fight to the end, in her own way, quietly, standing tall, and she'll know exactly when she's reached the limits of what she can tolerate. Until that moment, she'll remain unconditionally independent, and she'll acquiesce when the good Lord comes for her.

Grey faces get off and grey faces get on at the Hohenschönhauser Strasse / Weissenseer Weg stop. Some are perfectly made-up; their owners have painted over their tiredness. At Altenhofer Strasse we enter the world of eleven-storey blocks and giant leafy car parks. On we go, dead straight heading east, parallel with Landsberger Allee, the wide, seven-mile-long arterial road with its street numbers that go up to 576. The sky becomes wider. A tall man with a checked flat cap gets on at Zechliner Strasse. Could almost be Eberhard Pietsch.

Eberhard Pietsch has been sitting in his new armchair. He still brings me a mini bottle of sparkling wine, he still explains the world to me from on high and he still asks if I want to have sex with him. The number of his sexual conquests is stagnating at fifty-one, but the number of hikes with his cardiac rehab group has gone up from forty-three to forty-nine. When he next comes, I'll congratulate Herr Pietsch on the fiftieth hike he's planned and successfully accomplished.

Frau Guse no longer cooks, not even kassler on Saturdays. Every morning, a young man from a catering company brings her a hot lunch in an insulated box. Frau Guse joyfully devotes herself to studying the following week's menu and she puts a cross against the dishes she chooses. If she has money left over, she gives it to her children, all in their sixties.

A few months ago, Frau Huth rang to cancel her double appointment, saying that her husband was in hospital and she was visiting him every day. I haven't heard from them since. Maybe Herr Huth has died. Maybe he's now lying where Herr Paulke lies, in the Marzahn Park Cemetery. Maybe I'll never see Herr and Frau Huth again. Once, when we were talking about her own illnesses, which also needed treating, Frau Huth said, 'You have to make a choice.' Then she took her husband's hand. I don't know what Frau Huth will do if Herr Huth is no more. Whether Frau Huth can do what Frau Janusch has done.

Frau Janusch has had her glaucoma operated on at last. Here, we call it *Grüner Star* – *grün* means 'green' and *Star* comes from an old word for 'stare', although it can also mean 'starling'. She laughed until she cried when I asked if, during the operation, her green starling had turned out to be a green tody. Frau Janusch is coming to see me tomorrow at 2 p.m. She'll be able to tell me all about her minibreak in Ahrenshoop – it's the first time she's been there without her husband.

The M6 purrs along the track. Genslerstrasse, Arendsweg, Schalkauer Strasse. To the left, *plattenbau* housing; to the right, shopping temples. Höffner for furniture. Globus Baumarkt for DIY. The Globus garden centre for plants. The sun's rising behind IKEA. Today will be a clear, cold winter's day under a blue sky. I fish the salon key out of my rucksack and put it in my coat pocket.

The Nolls have got new hairstyles. The wound on Old Frau Noll's fontanelle has healed and the scab has come off. The hairdresser cut her white fluff short. Last time, when Old Frau Noll was once again sitting at Flocke's manicure table with her back hunched and her hands in the hand bath, she suddenly whipped her feet left and right, alternating, tap-tap-tap-tap, perfectly in time to 'Shape of You', an Ed Sheeran song which was tinkling softly from Flocke's radio. She can't be that deaf, I thought with a grin. She'll easily make it to a hundred.

Herr Hübner sometimes shuffles past the salon in his misshapen Crocs. I've stopped saying hello, because he never says it back.

When Frau Blumeier flew to London with Lutz for the weekend, she ended up in hospital. Kidney stones. Since then, she's been under constant surveillance and has to measure how much she drinks and how much she excretes, and she's been diagnosed with a kink in her urethra. It's irritating, and she often needs to have a urinary catheter put in. She wheeled up to me for a quick chat outside the salon and laughed when she said, 'Lutz keeps moaning about it. Everyone's gawping at me down there and he doesn't get a look-in!'

The M6 passes the Georg Knorr business park and leans into an elegant curve to the left, before taking a right turn for Marzahn S-Bahn station. I look over to the old S-Bahn bridge that leads to the cemetery. The shopping centre is still closed. I travel a little further, then I get off. The wind is whistling. The winter air stings my nose. Intense Marzahn weather. I cross over the tracks and tilt my head back, struck as always by the sense of being dwarfed by the eighteen storeys bearing down on the salon. Inside, I take my sandwiches and the cake to the kitchen, make myself a coffee, put on my white work clothes and get the chiropody room ready. I sit behind the reception desk with my mug and study the diary. No changes. My first client, Carola Hattenhauer, nicknamed Hatti, still needs to work for another five years before she hits retirement and today she's starting work a little later. I'm starting work a little earlier, so that Hatti can have decent feet. At nine on the dot, she rings the doorbell. I hurry to the door, smile through the glass and turn the sign from 'Closed' (red) to 'Open' (green).

THE PEIRENE SUBSCRIPTION

Since 2011, Peirene Press has run a subscription service which has brought a world of translated literature to thousands of readers. We seek out great stories and original writing from across the globe, and work with the best translators to bring these books into English – before sending each one to our subscribers, six to eight weeks ahead of publication. All of our novellas are beautifully designed collectible paperback editions, printed in the UK using sustainable materials.

Join our reading community today and subscribe to receive three translated novellas a year, as well as invitations to events and launch parties and discounts on all our titles. We also offer a gift subscription, so you can share your literary discoveries with friends and family.

A one-year subscription costs £35, including UK shipping. International postage costs apply.

www.peirenepress.com/subscribe

'The foreign literature specialist'

The Sunday Times

'A class act'

The Guardian

PEIRENE | STEVNS
TRANSLATION PRIZE

The Peirene Stevns Translation Prize was launched in 2018 to support up-and-coming translators.

Open to all translators without a published novel, this prize looks to award great translation and to offer new ways of entry into the world of professional translation.

The winner receives a £3,500 commission to translate a text selected by Peirene Press, the opportunity to spend two months at a retreat in the Pyrenees and a dedicated one-on-one mentorship throughout the translation process.

The Peirene Stevns Prize focuses on a different language each year and opens to submissions from October to January.

With thanks to Martha Stevns, without whom this prize would not be possible.